Presents:

BETTER MEMORY NOW

Memory Training Tips to Creatively Learn Anything Quickly

By Luis Angel Echeverria
Memory Master Champion on Superhuman
#1 Best Selling Author &
Memory Coach with AE Mind at
www.AEMind.com

Copyright © 2016 by AE Mind. All Rights Reserved
The **images** used in the *Better Memory Now* book were **licensed** from ShutterStock.com.

No part of this publication may be reproduced, stored in retrieval system, or transmitted in any form or by any means, electronic, mechanical, photocopying, recording, without the direct consent of AE Mind and Luis Angel Echeverria.

YOUR GIFTS

As a bonus, you'll be the first to get my latest **Free Memory Training Videos** and Content to help you with your ongoing continued memory improvement education!

Download Here:
www.BetterMemoryBook.com/Master

CONTACT

Learn more about Luis Angel's "Better Memory Now" programs and other Memory Training material for Professionals, Students, Memory Athletes, and Everyone Else, by going to:

www.AEMind.com

SOCIAL

YT: Youtube.com/AEMindMemory
FB: Facebook.com/AEMind1
IG: AE.Mind
Twitter: @AEMind
SnapChat: AEMind

Email: LuisAngel@AEMind.com

TESTIMONIAL

What others say about Luis Angel and The AE Mind: Better Memory Now System

Nathan Brais
Director of Student Life at Coastline College
"I just want to give a big shout out to Luis Angel Echeverria. Thank you so much for coming to our event. You're awesome, with a close to 500 students and staff here. You did 2 memory workshops for us, which the students were really impressed by, and I really appreciate you also doing our keynote address.
Luis is engaging and he's also great with students. He has a very energetic presence and I highly recommend him for any of your school events that you may be having for high school or for college group."

DANNY BELTRAN
AE Mind Memory Athlete and Student at UC Irvine.
"Joining the AE Mind team has been one of the best decisions I've ever made. **I was taught to memorize so many things without having to tear my head apart and it is so useful in academics**, not to mention **everyday life**. Luis is a great mentor and coach. Without him I wouldn't be in the position I'm in now. Thanks Luis for everything!"

KASSANDRA CEJA
AE Mind Memory Athlete and Student at UC Irvine
"Meeting Luis and joining the AE Mind Team has been a great experience. Not only did we get the chance to compete in the memory competition in New York, but we also learned skills that helped us memorize material for our academic courses. **We also got the opportunity to learn strategies that would benefit us with our future careers**. Being on the team we learned lots of skills, it opened our doors to many new opportunities, we got to meet many inspiring people, and it was overall one of the best decisions I have made."

THANK YOU

1st and Foremost, GOD and Mom!
&
Everyone Who Helped Me along the way to achieving my goals!

Better Memory Now

CONTENTS

ABOUT LUIS ANGEL viii
CONTRIBUTION ix
GETTING STARTED RIGHT x

SECTION I – AE MIND SYSTEM 1
   Chapter 1 – Hi! My name is Luis Angel & My Memory Sucked 2
   Chapter 2 – Location 12
   Chapter 3 – Visualize 16
   Chapter 4 – Review 22

SECTION II – POSITIVE MIND FOR SUCCESS 29
   Chapter 5 – Mindset 30
   Chapter 6 – Goals, Block Time, and Scheduling 35
   Chapter 7 – Focus and Health 39

SECTION III – MEMORY TRAINING 53
   Chapter 8 – More Locations = More Storage 54
   Chapter 9 – Names and Faces 63
   Chapter 10 – Numbers: The Basics 89
   Chapter 11 – Numbers: Double Digits 103
   Chapter 12 – Everyday Memory 131
   Chapter 13 – Accelerated Learning and Education 141

SECTION IV – MEMORY ATHLETES 155
   Chapter 14 – Memory Competitions 156
   Chapter 15 – Cards 167
   Chapter 16 – Words 175
   Chapter 17 – Numbers: Binary, New System, and Dates 180
   Chapter 18 – Names and Faces: Competition 188

Thank You 195
Contact 196

ABOUT LUIS ANGEL

- **1st Memory Master Champion on FOX's Superhuman**
- **Founder** and Main Memory Coach at AE Mind | Accelerated Empowered Mind
- **Competed** in the USA Memory Championship

- **Was the Youngest American** to Compete in the World Memory Championship with TEAM USA
- **Memorize: 120 Digit Number in 5 Minutes,**
- **Coached the AE Mind Memory Team** to a 1st Place Medal in the Numbers event at the USA Memory Championship
- **Started AE Mind Memory Clubs** in Los Angeles High Schools and in Universities such as UC Irvine and UC Santa Barbara.
- **Speaker** for Schools, Organizations, and Companies to help students and professionals have a "Better Memory Now"
- **Author and Creator of the AE Mind:** *Better Memory Now* **Series**

CONTRIBUTION

As someone who grew up in government-subsidized housing, on food stamps, and in an area with a lot of gang activity (never participated, but witnessed a lot of it around him), Luis Angel knows what it's like to have to go through struggle in life.

That's why Luis Angel loves contributing to help make the lives of those in need better in whichever way that he can.

GIVE BACK TUESDAY
Along with Living Waters and Countless of Amazing Volunteers, Luis Angel helps feed the homeless and families in need every Tuesday in the City of Santa Ana in Southern California.

FEED FAMILIES EVENT
Luis Angel has also partnered with Dion Jaffee, Bell High School, and several friends who donate to the cause to Feed Families every year for Thanksgiving!

A portion of the proceeds from the AE Mind Better Memory Now Live Events, Courses, and Books goes to continuing our Contribution Efforts!

Thank You in Advance for Your Contribution to the Cause!

GETTING STARTED RIGHT

Remember that this entire process is going to be a partnership. I have gone to many seminars and read many books where the speaker or author does a one-way interaction with the audience and expects them to be experts in that topic when they're done.

That's not how accelerated learning works.

At every single one of my seminars or events, whether I'm teaching a group of thousands of people or just doing a one-on-one training, the way that I teach is very interactive. I teach you how to be a creative story teller in order to memorize information through my own examples, and then you go ahead and create your own stories to help you memorize new material.

So, get ready to stretch your mind. Be like a parachute and allow your mind to work by being open to the ideas presented in this book. They have been tested all over the world by the best memorizers and they simply work when I applied correctly.

HONEST REVIEW

I love seeing the transformation that people go through when they learn this system, and I would be extremely grateful if you helped contribute to that transformation.

When you get a chance, if you could take about a minute or two to go to the Better Memory Now Book Page and leave a Review, you will truly be helping to improve the lives of thousands of people who struggle with their memory.

Thank You in Advance!

Other than that, let the show begin!

Enjoy, and Much Success on your journey to have an AE Mind!

(Copyright/Legal Info Because all of the images used in this book are licensed images, meaning we purchased the rights to use the images in this book, we must let you know that the images used in this book cannot be reproduced, stored in a retrieval system, or transmitted in any form or by any means, electronic, mechanical, photocopying, recording, without our direct consent. If you would like to get the licenses to use these images, please go to: www.ShutterStock.com.)

Thank you for understanding.

Section I
THE AE MIND MEMORY SYSTEM

Chapter 1
Hi! My name is Luis Angel and My Memory Sucked!

He stood there. Sweat profusely dripping down his forehead. In slow motion, a single drop rolled all the way down the edge of his face as he blinked ever so slowly. Tiiiiccccckkkkk. Toccccckkkkk. The second's hand sluggishly turned on the cat shaped clock on the wall. The aroma of burning ashes filled the room and entered through his nostrils. Jeff knew that he only had move to make and if he chose between the wrong colors then it would be game over. He had everything riding on choosing between the red or the green one.

A quick flash of a movie that he had just seen ran through his mind. The good guy chose the wrong wire to cut and the bomb detonated instantly. Although it wasn't the exact same situation, could this be Jeff's fate?

"Hurry babe, you don't have much time left." Janice said in a shivering and worried tone.

"I know honey, I just can't remember exactly which color was the right one." Jeff exclaimed.

A quick "eenie, meenie, miney, mo" chant cycled through his thoughts. He hit the red one...

"Jeeeefffff! What did you do? That was the wrong..." Janice yelled, but it was too late. Their fate was set.

Jeff and Janice lost the game of Simon which requires the user to memorize a pattern of blinking colored lights. He lost because of his lack of abilities to fully focus and remember a simple color scheme.

"Better luck next time guys, hahaha" John yelled out as the rest of the game night group continued to make s'mores on the stove.

Here's the thing, Bryan/Brenda (I like to give names to people that I haven't met yet. Actually, when I was in New York riding the subway, I was giving random names to people that were sitting near me and using the memory techniques that I'm going to teach you in this book to memorize their fake names. Sorry, this was a long side note. Let's continue...), memory is a fundamental part of our everyday existence. I know that experiences like the story above happen to people all the time; whether it's in a very serious situation that can potentially lead to a distraught outcome, or a fun and playful setting where you cause your team to lose because you forgot a pattern that you needed to memorize. The act of forgetting can trigger one of the most painful emotions that a person can feel.

On the flip side of this, don't you feel a sense of euphoria when you are able to successfully recall something important. Maybe it was the correct answers to a test, or perhaps it was the name of that special person that you met the previous week. We love it when we are able to remember things that are near and dear to us and hate it when we struggle with our memory.

Throughout the last several years of me improving my own memory and helping individuals achieve their goals of being able to learn faster and remember better, I've come across this pattern of limiting beliefs that people have about themselves. Most individuals raise their hands when I ask the following question during my Better Memory Now Live Events, "Who here believes that they have either a terrible memory or would love it if they could better remember even just day to day tasks?" From students to business professionals, people from all ages want to learn the secret formula on how to improve their memory and they want it NOW!

Well if you are one of those individuals who fits into that category then you're in luck because I'm about to release the magic sauce, RIGHT NOW!

The Key to Memorization is... VISUALIZATION!

That's it.
Simple.
Easy.
Done.

There is a catch. You see I compete all over the world in memory competitions and every one of my memory athlete friends will tell you that what they do to memorize a large amount of information in a short period of time, is that they visualize and create quirky stories in order to remember that info. To be one of the best memorizers however, the requirements are that you need to practice consistently. You don't take an easy fix pill or someone waves a magic wand over your head and all of a sudden you're reciting the first 1000 digits of pi. You need to put in some effort into taking this simple to learn concept and being able to use it to remember, say your grocery list.

This book is designed to take you from an absolute beginner of knowing how to memorize to being able to compete in an international memory competition if you so wish to pursue that. But even if you just want to stop at being able to remember the names of the people that you meet, you can definitely do that and you will see huge improvements in your ability to remember and recall names, faces, and more!

My response to the question of "can ANYONE learn how to do this?" is always that as long as the person doesn't have any serious physical brain disabilities or disorders, then of course the answer is "YES!" Certain individuals have had serious brain trauma that impairs them from fully being able to embrace the techniques taught here, but the majority of the people that approach this with an open mind can definitely use the memory techniques to memorize and learn any information at an accelerated rate. I've worked with people that have ADHD, focus problems, dyslexia, early onset signs of dementia, and even individuals that are blind, and every one of them have had success with being able to improve their memory skills. I myself was diagnosed with Attention Deficit Disorder and have been able to turn that situation around after being introduced to this world of competitive memorization.

THE LUIS ANGEL STORY

When I raised the trophy as the first memory master champion on the first episode of Superhuman, I couldn't hold back the tears that soon were flowing out of my eyes and going down my cheeks as I thought back to all the struggles that I had up to that point. Just a few years prior to this moment, my grades were suffering greatly in school, I almost getting fired from my job, and was not a good place with my everyday life. Everything around me was going in a downward spiral in which I felt like I had no control over.

At school, I had a 1.0 GPA my freshman year, and graduated by having a 1.75 GPA my senior year in high school. I had to repeat several classes in between those years because my brain was just not retaining the information that it needed to. I couldn't focus, I couldn't concentrate, and I couldn't remember all that well. When I finally did graduate, I thought that things were going to be different in college. That wasn't the case, because I ended up getting kicked out of school for my continued efforts of not doing great in my classes.

I was on the verge of getting fired from my job at a satellite TV company because of my forgetfulness. I would constantly lose my tools and would fail to remember the procedures of installing the satellite dishes on people's homes. There were plenty of times when the following happened. I would be up on a roof to get ready to drill the dish onto the black tar that I had just placed on top of the shingles, when I would realize that I was missing a bolt. I would go down the ladder while carrying my heavy tool belt and go straight to the van. Along the way, something must have happened to my train of thought because as soon as I opened the van's door I would wonder what I was supposed to get. I would go back up to the top of the house to see if I could get a trigger to remind me and then it would hit me. "I need a bolt, I need a bolt, I need a bolt..." I kept repeating to myself over and over again. This instance and several others were making me cost the company a lot of money and they had already given me tons of warnings to improve my ability to perform the tasks at hand or face the ultimate consequence of getting the pink slip.

At home, things such as remembering whether I ate or not became a fixture for my everyday life. My mom would ask me at 3 PM on a Saturday after she got home from work, "mijo ya comiste/son did you eat?" I couldn't give her an answer because I honestly didn't remember. Another one of my favorites was walking into my room knowing that I was there to get something of importance and staring at the bed for a good 60 seconds only to realize that I had forgotten why I was in that room in the first place. Events like these were constant recurrences that I knew had to be stopped or at least dramatically tamed back several notches.

The last straw happened on an island off the coast of Southern California called, Catalina Island. I was there to install cable. When we go out to the island, we need to place all of the tools and equipment that we are going to need for each one of the jobs inside of a large plastic bin. We then board the ferry and travel afloat the pacific waters for 45 minutes. Well dummy me ended up leaving behind several tools and satellite dish parts that were required to complete each job. I remember sitting on a bench waiting the three hours until my ferry came to pick me up. I had just cancelled all of the jobs that I had for the day and was thinking to myself that I was getting fired. As I saw out onto the crashing waves, I felt like my world was also crashing down on me.
My mind just kept reviewing all of the negative situations that had

led me to this point. All of those times that I kept forgetting. All of those times that I couldn't remember something. Every single time that I lacked focus at school, work, and in my personal life. I was seeing all of the pain that this had cost me and how painful my life was going to be if I continue to remain stuck in the same pattern. I began to shed tears upon tears. My vision was blurry. I cried. I sobbed. I had pity. I had regret. I was a total mess.

"God help me find a solution to this misery!" I yelled out in my mind hoping that he would hear.

And then, it hit me. He answered my prayers because I instantly knew what I had to do.

There was a gentleman a few years back that did a seminar where he memorized the names of hundreds of people in the audience and repeated all of them from memory. He then taught everyone in attendance how to do what he had just done. I wasn't there, but my friend Dion was.

"D, I need to know that memory guy's name. Do you remember it?"

He told me, "yea it's Ron White."

As soon as I got home, I went online and got the memory course and went through it immediately. I quickly put the memory techniques to use and saw results right away. I was able to memorize a list of words in a matter of minutes. I memorized a long number and repeated it forward and backwards. I was able to remember the names of the people that I had met. More importantly, it helped me in every area of life that I was previously struggling with because of my memory problems. At school, I went from getting kicked out for a semester to getting straight A's. I went from almost getting fired from my job to getting a promotion and becoming the youngest technician to hold that new position at my office. I went from forgetting the basics at home, to competing all over the world in memory competitions. This is what led me to compete in the Superhuman show and become the 1st Memory Master Champion!

I have also trained other students who have gone on to compete in memory competitions and they have taken home Gold in national events. All of my students that have graduated from high school are now attending high ranking universities here in California. One of the schools that I work with, Bell High School, was featured with me on the show Superhuman. I am much more proud of what they have achieved than what I did, because it shows that with a little bit of hard work anyone can learn how to use these memory techniques in every area of life!

Visualize This

You're walking up to a young lady with curly hair at a party and you two exchange names. She tells you that her name is Paris S. and that she is from Chicago Illinois. You instantly picture the Eiffel Tower with snakes wrapped around it trying to reach a deep-dish Chicago style pizza at the top of her Paris' curly hair.

Why are you seeing all of this?

Because you have learned that the Key to Memorization is Visualization and that the best way to remember something important, is to create a quirky visual story. All of the top memory athletes from around the world use this same technique in international memory championships. I've competed alongside them in several of the competitions. One in particular made me the first Memory Master Champion on the hit TV show, Superhuman!

I was sitting on the chair with my hands covering my face as I prayed for a calm and clear mind because I knew that millions of people were going to be watching from home. When my hands came down, the image flashed on the large screen. A young lady

with curly hair who I had seen earlier that day. She was one of over 100 audience members which I had to memorize the personal information of, prior to me heading out and taking center stage. I had to memorize their first name, last name initial, hometown (city, state), and a feature about them. As I looked at her face on the screen, my brain immediately scanned through the hundreds of stories that I created to help me remember the 500+ pieces of information. There were a few ladies in the audience with curly hair, but this one was unique. As I waved my hands around in the air to help me get a clearer picture and narrow down her name and hometown, it hit me!
"Paris S. from Chicago, Illinois," I told the Superhuman host, Kal Penn.

"Are you sure?" he says.

"Sure he's sure," yells out Mike Tyson. "That's why he's in that chair!"

I smiled and told Kal to lock in that answer.

As she stood up from out in the audience, she says, "my name is Paris S. and I'm from Chicago, Illinois."

I jumped up with sheer excitement and joy! And as I continued to get every single one of these correctly, I became very grateful that these memory techniques came into my life. I hugged my mom, my entire family, my friend's Dion and Feibi, the host, the panelist, all of the contestants, and of course my mentor Ron White.

He was on the show with me and also nailed his challenge of quickly memorizing a ton of numbers, names, faces, and facts about the people that he met. I got real emotional as I thanked him for everything that he had done for me and for teaching this kid from the LA County city of La Puente, how to use his full mind's power to achieve what seemed impossible a few years earlier. In order to get over my struggles in school and in life, he taught me that I needed to just let my creativity flow through as I reviewed the information that I wanted to remember.

I am here to be that guiding hand for you as you embark on this journey of unlocking the true power of your mind's ability to hold onto information. Just as the gift was given to me by my mentor, I am going to share that gift with you. Realize that if you were able to remember that Eiffel Tower with snakes and a deep-dish Chicago pizza, then you too can become a memory master!

The AE Mind Memory System is simple to learn and easy to master with practice.

There are three steps that you need to remember.

1. Location
2. Visualize
3. Review

I will spend this first section teaching you how each one of these three steps work and why it is crucial for long term memory retention.

> Faith is taking the first step even when you don't see the whole staircase.
>
> —Martin Luther King Jr.

Chapter 2
Location

At the Australian Memory Championship, I got the Gold Medal position in cards by memorizing a full deck in 2 minutes. I did this by creating several stories very quickly along a path in my mind. As I was shuffling through the cards, I visualized my mom hugging a bone near my living room's window. I saw Scooby Doo biting a Tesla Car on a painting I have on the wall. Then Captain America was slinging his shield and slicing a lime on my couch. This kept going on until I created 26 stories along the entire living room. I then recalled the cards in perfect order by translating those images into the cards. So the ace of hearts (mom) and the 9 of hearts (bone) were my first two cards. Then came the 2 of spades (Scooby), 7 of diamonds (Tesla), 10 of spades (Captain America), 5 of clubs (lime), and so on…

Let's start off with laying down the foundation for being able to memorize anything that you want to remember along a sequential order. We need to create our first set of mental locations in order for that to happen.

I have over 1000 locations, but that's just because I compete in international memory competitions. You don't need to do that to see the immediate benefits of this memory system. Let's start off with your first 10 locations.

These are going to be locations in which you are already very familiar with. They are going to be in your home. You don't have to be physically present or near the locations in order to use them for your mental journeys. Just use your imagination and visualize yourself at these spots.

So first, see yourself in the living room. Look around at all of the different objects, furniture, items, etc… What do you see here? Do you see a couch, a lamp, a TV? How about a rug, a coffee table, a nightstand? See in your mind's eye all of the various things that you have in the living room. Now let's move on to the next room in your home.

What's the next room or area with different items in it, near the living room? My second room is the bathroom. The specific locations that I chose in the bathroom are, the toilet, the medicine cabinet, shower, a stand, and a towel rack. What do you see in this 2nd room of yours? Look around the room and notice anything large, medium size and small.

Now that we saw some items in each room, let's go ahead and number 5 locations in each room.

Using the boxes below, or on a separate sheet of paper, list 5 things that you see in each room going clockwise. Don't jump around. Meaning if your first location is the couch and the TV is on the complete opposite end of the room, don't label the TV as number 2. Maybe save it for your 5th location. Choose something to the right of the couch as your 2nd location instead.

MY SAMPLE LOCATIONS:

Living Room	Bathroom
1. Couch	6. Toilet
2. Table	7. Medicine Cabinet
3. Mirror	8. Shower
4. Heater	9. Clothes Stand
5. TV	10. Towel Rack

Your First 10 Location:

Room 1: _____   Room 2: _____

1. _____   6. _____
2. _____   7. _____
3. _____   8. _____
4. _____   9. _____
5. _____   10. _____

Now go over these 10 locations several times until you can call them out by number. What's location number 1? What about number 4? And your 8th location is? How about the 10th one? Say them forwards and backwards a few times until you can recall this sequence without thinking too much about it.

Once you have done that, let's move on to the fun step of actually memorizing things using these mental locations or your first journey.

> *It is in your moments of decision that your destiny is shaped.*
>
> —Tony Robbins

Chapter 3
Visualize

The power of visualization. Olympians use it to get themselves in the right state of mind before going out to practice or competition. Phil Jackson was said to have used it with all of his players from Michael Jordan and the Chicago Bulls, to Kobe Bryant and the Lakers. Albert Einstein used to visualize all of his formulas and thought experiments in his mind before actually putting pen to paper. Visualization is powerful and we are going to use this power of your mind to remember a simple list of 10 things.

These 10 items all have a specific meaning which I will get into full detail in a later chapter. For now, let's just go ahead and visualize these 10 things.

We'll break them apart into chunks of 5 to make it easier to remember.

I want you to picture a **Hat** being thrown on the first location in your living room. Personify the hat and see it dancing on the 1st location. Add music to the image, add as many senses as you can. The stronger the visual, the easier that it will be for you to recall the item later on.

On the second location, I want you to see **Honey** being squirted all over the location. Feel how sticky it is and even taste it by licking that entire location.

The third item will be a piece of **Ham**. See the ham being sliced onto the third location. Maybe you start making ham sandwiches on this location.

For the fourth object, I want you to picture an **Hour Glass** being broken on that 4th location with glass and sand spread out everywhere.

The fifth one is going to be **Hail**. Picture an icy hail storm pounding down hard on your fifth location. How does it sound like? How does it feel when you rub that location that has all the hail on it?

Now, close your eyes and see all five of these items interacting with the five locations that you placed them on. Are they on there pretty tightly sealed? If you are having trouble seeing some of the objects, make sure you allow your creativity to flow and add more action in order to make the visual triggers more memorable.

I was recently doing a live YouTube memory training session where I memorized a 50 spoken digit number and recalled it perfectly on my AE Mind Memory channel, and one of the viewers asked me about how I was able to do it without having a lapse in memory. I told him that it was because I added a lot of action between the images for my numbers and the location. I had a piece of wood on my table and I told him to imagine as if this was one of the locations along his mental journey. I then pulled out a model sized Big Ben clock tower that I got when I competed at the World Memory Championship with Team USA back in 2012.

I told him to pretend as if Big Ben was your image representation for the number 99. If you just imagine Big Ben erect on this slab of wood without adding any extra action to the story and you had to memorize a 100 digit number, you are going to have a hard time during the recall period. Because by the time you had to recall that entire number and you got to that location of the piece of wood, then you might confuse the object that was standing on it with something else. You might mistake it with The Leaning Tower of Pisa or another such tower.

What you want to do to avoid this issue, is to add a lot of action. I like to personify the objects that I'm memorizing. So perhaps see Big Ben breakdancing on the wood board and doing a head spin. Hear the sound of the crowd around it as he busts his moves. Listen to the cheers. "Go Big Ben, Go Big Ben, Go!" This helps to connect multiple neurons in your brain as you memorize the information and will help ease the process of recalling the info. Once you practice doing this several times, this sequence will become easier and faster. You will see the entire visual story come to life in milliseconds in your mind.

Now, let's do the next 5 images. I will give the objects to you and I want you to create the visual triggers to help you memorize them. **Remember to Trust Your Brain's Ability to Be Creative!!**

On your sixth location, picture a **Hash Brown**. The seventh location will feature a pirate **Hook**. The next one is a horse's **Hoof**. Followed by the ninth one being a hula **Hoop**. Then the last location will have a **House** doing something on top of it.

Close your eyes and visualize these 5 objects interacting with your locations. Add more action to them to make them more memorable.

Now go ahead and write down the 10 things that we memorized on the locations, from memory. Check your answers afterwards:

1. _____
2. _____
3. _____
4. _____
5. _____
6. _____
7. _____
8. _____
9. _____
10. _____

Here are the answers:

1. Hat
2. Honey
3. Ham
4. Hour Glass
5. Hail
6. Hash Brown
7. Hook
8. Hoof
9. Hoop
10. House

How many did you get correct? If the stories were strong enough, then you should have gotten all of them correct. Remember that the Key to Memorization is Visualization and that our brain learns best when it can clearly see the information. It also loves it when it gets entertained, so adding a lot of action between the objects and the locations will make these stories stand out and you will find it easier to recall the information later on.

For long term memory to kick in, there is one more step that we need to do. That is the Review process.

> You can't use up creativity. The more you use, the more you have.
>
> —Maya Angelou

Chapter 4
Review

At the World Memory Championship in China, I was competing alongside Team USA when I memorized and perfectly recalled a 120 digit number in a 5 minutes. If you were to ask me today to repeat that number back to you, I would say, "well there was a 2 in there somewhere." I can't recall the entire sequence of numbers anymore because I told my brain that it wasn't important to retain that piece of information after the competition was over with. In order for this to happen, you simply don't strengthen the neuronic connections in your brain by not reviewing the info.

On the contrary, if you were to ask me right now to recite the first few hundred digits of pi, I would say "3.1415926535897932 38..." The reason why I could do this with ease, is because I have reviewed that sequence of numbers long after the initial memorization period. It has been cemented into my long term memory and should forever be there because I repeat a good portion of it during my memory improvement shows at high schools and colleges.

Back in the day, we needed to rely on our memory to remember phone numbers because smart phones weren't a thing yet. I still remember our old home phone number: 626-864-0782 (I wouldn't recommend for you to dial that number as I have no clue who owns it anymore). We had to force ourselves to ask our brains to pull our home's, mom's, or friend's phone number instead of asking Siri to do it for us. We repeated those numbers so much that they were ingrained into our unconscious mind until we were able to say them without having to consciously think about the number. That's the difference maker between short term and long term memory.

Before I get into the actual neuroscience behind why reviewing is so important, let's go ahead and review the 10 things that we memorized earlier. You don't have to write anything down right now, but just go ahead and after you're done reading these directions, close your eyes, take a deep breath, clear your mind, and visualize the ten pictures that we created along the route in our mind. See if you can visualize all of them.

How'd you do?
Were you able to see them pretty clearly?

That's what I like to do when I review any piece of information that I want to remember for a longer period of time. I memorize chunks of data at a time, I then pause and close my eyes to review and strengthen the images that I created.

Reviewing = Long Term Memory.

In the book "The Other Brain," Dr. Douglas Fields talks about how when we review something, brain cells called glial cells help support the neurons to fire off much more quickly the next time that you want to retrieve that information. More specifically, these glial cells shoot off something called myelin onto the neurons when they send electrical signals down the axons and then the terminals shoot off neurotransmitters to the receiving end of another neuron (the dendrites).

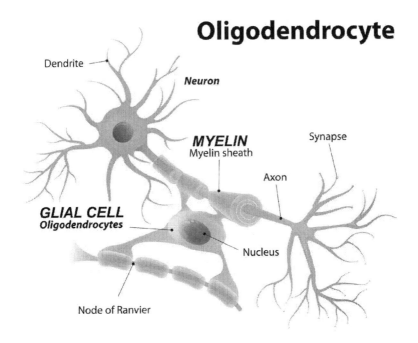

Let me explain the importance of this process through a metaphor.

As you know from reading the Intro section, I used to work for a satellite TV company. My job was to install the customer's cable and make sure that everything was running smoothly before I left. Meaning they needed to be able to see their favorite TV channels and shows before it was time for me to pack up and go to my next job.

The way that they received a pretty HD picture on their TV set was because the cable connected to the back of the receiver box was getting a digital signal coming from the satellite dish that converted another signal coming from the actual satellites floating hundreds of miles up in space.

Amazing, I know!

So what carries this electrical signal from the satellite dish, through the cable, and onto the receiver? It's a copper wire only about a few millimeters thick. It's probably as thick as an unfolded paperclip.

So why is it that the actual cable that you see hooked up to the back of your TV cable box is much thicker than what it should be? This is because in order for the signal to flow smoothly and in a quick manner from one end to the other without getting any signal loss, the copper wire needs to be wrapped with insulation. There are actually several layers of insulation, as you see below.

I've had to go to hundreds of troubleshooting service calls at customers' houses during my stint as a cable installer, and one of the biggest problems was that the dog had chewed up the cable. They had cut through the insulation, leaving the copper cable exposed and not allowing the electrical signal to reach the cable box.

Now with that knowledge in your brain, let's apply this to how our neurons work.

Imagine that the axon, which carries the electrical signal, is the copper cable. The insulation is the myelin that wraps around the axon.

Without any or perhaps just a thin layer of myelin, the neurons don't fire off as effectively and efficiently as they should. However, when you repeatedly fire off those neurons by reviewing the information that you want to memorize and learn, the glial cells pick up on that and send myelin to wrap around the axon.

Again, Reviewing = Long Term Memory.

As an FYI, did you know that when they were looking at Albert Einstein's brain, the neuroscientists couldn't see any size difference between his brain and an average brain?

What they did see that was different was the amount of white matter in his brain. The white matter is the myelin that wraps around the neurons. He had a lot more white matter than the average human brain.

Albert Einstein was known to visualize or create thought experiments in his mind when he wanted to solve a problem.

This is just something to consider when going through this process of Visualizing in order to Memorize.

Now that you know the memorizing systems, let's put this into practice.

> "For I know the plans I have for you," declares the Lord, "plans to prosper you and not to harm you, plans to give you hope and a future."
>
> —Jeremiah 29:11

Section II
POSITIVE MIND FOR SUCCESS

Chapter 5
Mindset

"I'm Stupid, I'm Dumb, I Suck at School, I Forget Easily, I Can't Read, I Can't Focus, I Can't Learn Anything, I Can't, I Can't, I Can't..."

These and many more limiting beliefs used to clog my mind whenever I would enter the classroom, sit down on my chair, set my books on top of the desk, and pretend to pay attention to the teacher. My mind would start wandering off into another dimension and think about everything else but what I was supposed to be focusing on, which was learning the material at hand. I would think about what I was going to eat later on that day, the TV show I was going to watch (the Real World on MTV), the pretty girl in 4th period that I liked but was too scared to talk to. All of these things would be circling around my thought bubble because of the brick wall that I created for myself by saying all of those negative things.

In the movie, *The Pursuit of Happyness*, Will Smith is playing basketball with his son Jayden when Will tells him to not get his hopes up about being a successful basketball player. That because he wasn't able to be good at sports, that his kids more than likely won't be any good at sports either. Jayden, feeling like his dreams had been shattered, gets the ball and places it into a plastic bag. At that point Will realizes what he had done and walks over to his son, "don't ever let someone tell you that you can't do something, not even me."

I took this line to heart and gave it a little twist. Many times when we're trying to do something and we're having a hard time figuring it out, we might have voices telling us to give up and that we're not good enough. Those voices aren't necessarily always external ones. They often come from within. We tell ourselves to give up. We tell ourselves that we're never going to be successful. We say "you suck, you can't do this, you'll never be good, they could do this because they're gifted, but you have no gifts." All of these words are detrimental to moving forward on with being able to grasp a new idea in a timely manner.

I view these negative thoughts, both self-imposed and externally influenced comments, as bricks. Every time that you allow one of these negative thoughts to cement into your mind, you're stacking these bricks on top of each other to create a brick wall that blocks new information from easily flowing into your mind. This wall slows down dramatically the rate at which you are able to absorb information or completely stops it dead in its tracks when it bounces off of the wall. What you need to do is build a sledge hammer of positivity so that you can break down this wall. You want to say things such as, "I have been given an amazing gift of being able to absorb and retain knowledge quickly, I have a powerful and smart mind, I can get and stay focused at will…" so on and so forth. By countering those negative thoughts with positive ones, you are going to allow the flow of new information to get processed at an expedited rate compared to when you had that dark wall of negative thoughts preventing the information to flow easily.

Down below or on a separate sheet of paper, go ahead and write down some of the disempowering thoughts that you have allowed to circle around your mind in the past, and then cross them out and on the other side, write down as many empowering thoughts that you will now allow your mind to live in moving forward.

Disempowering	Empowering

Have you ever been inside of your car and you hear a new song being played on the radio and you're just not feeling that song? When this happens to me, I simply change the radio station. The next day when I listen to that original radio station, guess what happens. They start playing that new undesirable song again. The next action step is of course to change the station once again. A few days go by and what do you know, you're out at the store and you hear that song playing through the loud speakers. You have no choice now but to listen to it because you still need to get some shopping done. The next time that you hear that song again is in your friend's car because they really like it so they turn up the volume to full blast. At this point, you start to ease off of the "hate" pedal and start bobbing your head to the beat of the song. When you get back into your car the next day, you already know what the radio station is playing. The song comes on again and you start singing the main hook chorus. "Baby, Baby, Baby, ooooohhhh..." goes the Justin Bieber song, right.

At first, you're probably not going to be that confortable with telling yourself these new and empowering things that you wrote down. It's going to seem foreign to you and their will more than likely be skepticism from your self. You'll say that these new thoughts don't really represent who you are and that you're still not good enough. But what you MUST do is, rewire your framework of thinking by continuing to repeat the positive assertions about yourself. Be your own radio station and play these new tracks on repeat until you start to fully embrace and acknowledge them as truth. Because they are your new truth! You are Smart! You are a Genius! You can learn anything quickly!

> The roots of education are bitter, but the fruit is sweet.
>
> —Aristotle

Chapter 6
Goals, Block Time, and Scheduling

Now that you have secured a positive way of thinking for yourself, let's go ahead and set some goals for what you want to achieve after reading and going through this book. Remember that this is not about you passively consuming the contents of this Better Memory Now book, but instead it's about you actively engaging in the material so that you can absorb it quickly and implement it into your daily life. In order to get the most out of it, I highly encourage you to set some goals for yourself before moving forward.

When I first started out with learning how to memorize quickly, my biggest intention was to do well in school. To spend less time studying and more time enjoying the learning process. I feel like I have achieved that goal and then some.

What are your top 3 goals that you want to achieve once you complete this entire book and why do you want to achieve them?

Is it to be able to comprehend more of what you read? Is it to memorize a 100 digit number in a few minutes? Is it to memorize the names of all of the individuals at your next meeting? Is it to use this information to ace your next exam in class? What are those goals for you? These goals will help you to stay focused and alert as you're going through the material. Write them down here or on another sheet of paper.

Goals

Goal #1

_____
_____
_____

Why Must You Accomplish this Goal?

_____
_____
_____

Goal #2

_____
_____
_____

Why Must You Accomplish this Goal?

_____
_____
_____

Goal #3

_____
_____
_____

Why Must You Accomplish this Goal?

_____
_____
_____

Block Time and Scheduling

Another study tip for your success, is block time. Make sure to block time off from your schedule to solely dedicate it to you going through the exercises in this Better Memory Now book. Set a target time for you to go through the material and stick with that on a consistent basis. If all that you have is to spend 10 minutes a day going through these exercises, then block that off on your calendar and when the time arrives, sit down and make sure to only actively go through this material during that allotted time. If you can spare an hour a day, then obviously you will be done with this book much more quickly and can even faster apply what you have learned to helping you achieve your goals at a quicker rate. It's completely up to you as to how much time you want to allocate to the betterment of your memory. Just make sure that you set it and block off that time for your Memory Training.

I do this for every area of my life. I have blocked off time slots for my health and fitness, for business, social life, memory training, and more. I make sure that during that time, I only focus on that particular area of life as to not easily get distracted by the other things that I also have to do. You will train your brain to focus on the one thing at hand. We will get more into Focus and how you can strengthen your attention paying muscle in the next chapter. So go ahead and schedule in some time for your memory training for this next week.

> Every strike brings me closer to the next home run.
>
> —Babe Ruth

Chapter 7
Focus and Health

A few years ago when I was diagnosed with Attention Deficit Disorder and was given the "focus" pills by my doctor in order to help me with my lack of being able to pay attention, I had asked him if he would recommend for me to do meditation exercises to help me out. He told me that at this medical facility they only focus on giving out medication to help their patients with these symptoms.

But you see, I was never a fan of taking medication unless it was absolutely required and necessary in a life and death situation. Even though I lived in an area in Los Angeles where drugs and alcohol were a rite of passage for most of the kids out there, I never got into that scene. I disliked the idea of putting these foreign substances into my body in order to feel a certain way. That without them, we couldn't feel happy, joyful, ecstatic, energetic, and that we couldn't enjoy life. I didn't subscribe to that ideology.

So when I was given these pills to take, I had a hard fought battle with my mind about whether I should consume them or not. I was at a breaking point and was absolutely fed up with living the way that I was of always forgetting things and not being able to focus. I took the pills.

I still remember the first time that I took them. I had never been so focused in my entire life. If you have ever seen that movie "Limitless" where Bradley Cooper takes NZT for the first time and he feels as if he could now access his full mind's potential, that's exactly how I felt at the time. I walked into my dirty room and was disgusted at myself. I thought to myself, "who in their right mind would live in a place like this. So disorganized and so messy." I had clothes everywhere. I couldn't tell which were dirty and which were clean. I had stacks of dishes and cups in a corner section of my room. There were moldy things underneath my bed that to this day I still don't know what they were.

I remember walking over to my bed, lifting up my mattress, throwing it out into the living room and getting to work. I completely organized my room, cleaned every square inch of this place, and then went on to clean my mom's living room, kitchen, and bathroom. Throughout the entire time, I remember only thinking about what I was doing at that given point in time. I didn't think about anything else. After I was done, I felt a sense of comfort and completion. I sat back on my mom's couch and turned on the TV. I hardly ever watched television, but I wanted to fully test out these "focus" pills.

Growing up, I couldn't ever have conversations with my friends about the cartoons that we had seen on TV or a movie that we had just watched, because I couldn't remember most of the content that I had seen. So I let them do all of the talking.

I wanted to see if I could actually remember what I was watching, so I turned to the news station and noticed that my eyes were super zoomed in and wired to the TV screen. Everything in my peripheral view was just a total blur. The newscaster was talking about the stock market and how experts were predicting that an uptick in the market was about to happen in the next few days. I was engulfing all of the information as it was presented to me. I felt like I was becoming an expert in the stock market just by watching them talk about it on TV. I was able to recite most of what I learned while watching the news show the next day when I was talking to my classmates.

I took my next dosage the following day before going to school. This was where the real test was going to happen. I had already been kicked out of college for a semester for having bad grades. Was this going to help turn things around?

When I walked into class, I didn't have the same ultra focused feeling that I did the previous day, but I did feel more relaxed and mentally calm than before. Once again, I noticed my eyes locked into the teacher just like they did when I was watching the news. I was able to listen and absorb most of what the professor was saying and was by far one of the most pro-participation classes that I have ever had on my behalf. I was asking the right questions and even responding back with all of the right answers that the teacher wanted. I was in the moment and fully present on a mental level. There was a catch though.

When I picked up my pencil to take some notes, I felt my hand get very shaky. That's when I noticed that my heart was actually beating at an alarming fast pace. Other than my hand shaking, my body overall felt calm, but my heart felt like it was going to pop out of my chest. This frightened me.

I took the pills again the next day and what do you know, I was back to my old self of not being able to fully focus on the task at hand and my mind was easily wandering off into another world. The one quality that did persist was the jittery feeling and heart pounding sensation that I had previously felt. I didn't like this one bit. I emailed my doctor and his response was for me to double my dosage. He told me that my body had adapted to the prescription drugs very quickly and that I needed a higher dosage. I didn't like this at all. I wanted a different way to get the same effect that I was experiencing on the first day without it just being a temporary fix or a Band-Aid. I wanted to find a permanent solution to this issue.

I got the pills, opened up the bottle, and poured them all down the toilet. This was the only way to force myself to find a real solution that didn't involve me having to depend on external forces to help me achieve my goal of getting and staying focused at will and being able to remember things much better.

I turned to the memory program that my mentor taught and also turned to several other mind empowering individuals. People like

Tony Robbins who taught his students how to tap into their God given abilities and talents to achieve their outcomes. I leaned on individuals like my first mind coach, Nicholas Rave, who taught me how to access my mind's potential of "getting stuff done" and staying focused by practicing a few simple things. I watched video after video on YouTube where people would walk me through different visualization and meditation exercises to help me hone in on the skills of being focused. I went to Bikram or Hot Yoga sessions for 90 minutes at a time in order to completely clear out my mind and concentrate solely on the moves that the instructor was guiding us through.

All of this led me to discover the true power of all of our minds and the fact that not everyone that is diagnosed with these focus "diseases" and "conditions" need to depend on medication, drugs, and foreign bodily substances in order to practice the art of getting into flow. We all have the ability to go into our mind and achieve this sense of focus by doing certain tasks on a consistent basis. In a moment, I'll walk you through one of my favorite visualization focus exercises that I created several years ago and one that I still use to this date in order to help myself instantly get into a state of focus. For now I want to talk to you about a few things that I would highly recommend for you to look into in order to improve your ability to pay attention, concentrate, and focus at will. Again, these are recommendations based on changes that I've made personally. Since I'm not one, make sure that you consult with your medical doctor if you have further questions before trying some of these recommendations.

Healthy Eating

Our brain consumes most of the calories that we take in when compared to any other body part. If you feed your body foods that are not beneficial to your body's overall wellbeing, then your brain will also suffer the consequences of a poor diet. My diet growing up consisted of Hot Cheetos, french fries, burgers, pizza, and several other fried and processed foods. Fruits and vegetables were rarely a part of my daily consumption. Soda's such as Pepsi and Squirt were my two go to drinks. Candy and chocolate were a necessity for me. I couldn't go one week without eating Reese's Peanut Butter Cups. They were my favorite.

As I started learning more about how these foods that we eat play a vital role in the performance of our brain, I began to discover that eating all of those "foods" were a huge contributor to my Attention Deficit Disorder problems. My body and brain weren't receiving the right nutrients in order to perform at an optimal level. Some of the most essential nutrients that our body and brain need are things such as omega 3 (fish and flax seeds/oil) and omega 6 (nuts and seeds) fatty acids, oleic acid (avocado/oil), vitamin B12 (eggs), vitamin C (oranges), potassium (banana), and more. I started creating brain power boosting smoothie drinks with blueberries, strawberries, oranges, and other antioxidant rich fruits and veggies to help support overall brain function. Adding foods high in these nutrients will do wonders for your memory.

DRINK A LOT of WATER! This one is a huge must. Our body and our brain is primarily composed of that liquidity thing that also engulfs the majority of the Earth. If you get tired easily or notice yourself losing focus quickly, it can be because you're either dehydrated or on the verge of being dehydrated. Doctors highly recommend for you to drink several glasses of water throughout the day to keep yourself hydrated, and so do I.

Exercise

In "The Memory Cure" by Dr. Majid Fotuhi, he talks about the importance of physical exercise and what role that plays into improving our overall brain function. They performed various different studies where they found a direct correlation between exercise and brain growth. Specifically, there is a part of the brain called the hippocampus that is linked to long term memory and it literally grows when we do cardiovascular exercise. The production of BDNF (Brain Derived Neurotrophic Factor is also linked with long term memory) increases as well when someone has a proper exercise regimen. This is essentially a self medicated way of helping out your brain to perform better. If you want to see a mild increase in your brain's performance, then go out for brisk walks around your block a few times a week. If you want to see much more noticeable differences in your ability to increase your ability to retain information, then going out for jogs or runs will increase the size of the hippocampus and BDNF production at a faster rate.

Hot Yoga

If you've never tried Hot Yoga, and your doctor says that it is okay for you to do it, I would highly recommend for you to try it once. Every time that I go, I feel my mind totally cleansed and laser focused after the session is over. I go to Bikram Yoga where they turn up the heat for 90 minutes while we are guided to do Yoga poses by the instructor. During the first 10 minutes, my mind begins to think of all of the things that I need to do and my anxiety tries to control of my mind. This is where I let that part of my mind know that we are going to stick this through all the way to the end without checking my phone or worrying about any outside circumstances. My sole intention here is to focus on the yoga poses and follow the leadership of the yoga instructor. Throughout this process my body sweats out and soaks every inch my body and clothing attire that I have on. This is where the body and mind cleansing comes into play. What happens after is that that because I have gone through a rigorous process of staying focused on the task at hand for 90 minutes straight, I have conditioned my mind to do that for other tasks as well.

I remember the first time that I ever did hot yoga. It was during a time that I was having a hard time with writing an essay that I had due that next day. I couldn't stay focused and I kept getting distracted with watching YouTube videos or focusing on anything but that essay. I went in to the yoga studio and came out with an exact blueprint on how to go from start to finish on my essay. When I got home, what took me weeks to finally get started on, ended up only taking me a few hours to finish. As Tony Robbins says, it's not that it took the weeks, months, or years to make a decision, it took a second. It takes seconds or a single moment to decide whether you want to do something and keep doing it. Doing hot yoga lays a huge framework in your mind of what's possible to put your body and mind through and still come out alive and more importantly, extremely alert. Again, I would highly recommend for you to do hot yoga or even regular yoga for that matter, if you're medically able to.

Clear Mind Meditation

In the international memory competitions, we have long events. For up to an hour, we have to sit down and memorize as many decks of cards as we possibly can. The same goes for random digits of numbers. These events can be grueling if you're not mentally prepared for them. That's why I practice clear mind meditation. This is where I sit down, play some classical music, and do my best to completely think of nothing but a flash of light floating in front of. Whenever I stop seeing that flash of light and start allowing my mind to wander off, I know that my focus conditioning has begun to falter. I simply tell myself to bring my awareness and focus back to this flash of light.
When I first started doing this, I could only go about a minute before my mind would begin to wander. So the strategy that I used was to set a time limit for myself. I would do 1 minute meditation

sessions. Then increase it to 3 minutes. Then go up to 5 minutes. And every session after that, I would go up a few minutes until I was able to and actually wanted to do hour long meditation sessions.

Try it out for yourself. Set a goal of just doing 1-5 minute meditation sessions for a week straight. Then increase it until you can do 15-30 minute sessions without having your mind wander.

Guided Visualization

This is by far the most powerful task that I have ever done to help me with my ability to focus and pay attention. I learned about guided visualization from the mind empowerment courses events that I attended. This is where I learned the true power of the mind and how you can access past memories, create future paced memories, or simply use metaphorical stories to help you stay focused on the tasks at hand so that you can achieve your goals. Accessing past memories and anchoring the feelings that we felt in the past when we were in certain states of mind, is extremely helpful when we want to focus on something new.

I remember growing up I used to be heavily in a focused state of mind when I wanted to fix something. From fixing my computer that stopped working to fixing my remote controlled car, I would spend as much time as was possibly needed to make sure that the end result was a working piece of equipment. I called it the "whatever it takes" mindset. You stick with the task at hand and do whatever it takes to get the job done. If I took that approach to my studies in high school, I would have gotten much better results. Whenever I need to get something done now, I first visualize myself in those moments when I was hyper focused and allow those same feeling to surge through my body as if I were experiencing that situation right there and then.

Future pacing events means that you see the end result of the thing that you want accomplish. This is called results in advance in the mind empowerment and personal development world. You see all of the good that can come out of you accomplishing the task and also the bad that can come if you don't accomplish it. At Tony Robbins' Unleash The Power Within Event, he has us go through a process where we see all of our major goals being accomplished and also the worst possible scenarios that can happen if we don't accomplish them.

I remember seeing myself as a memory champion and what kind of satisfaction I had once I became that several years before it even happened on national TV. What I also saw was my mom still struggling financially, my future kids living under the same conditions that I grew up in, myself continuing to have a terrible memory, if I didn't focus on the issues and train extremely hard to become one of the best memorizers in the world. This is called the pain and pleasure principle. Attach both pain and pleasure to the goals that you want to accomplish, because this is what's going to help you to get focused quickly and stay focused for a longer period of time.

Creating metaphors to help you get and stay focused is also a really good way to help you do just that. I'll walk you through one of my favorite ones right now:

Race Track Visualization

Allow your mind right now to completely let go of any outside thoughts or distractions that might be clogging your mind from experiencing a total sense of inner peace and harmony. Many times when we can't focus on something that's very important for us to focus on, we tend to allow our minds to wander off into a completely different world where we lose ourselves and give in to mental distractions. This can lead to a chaotic spiral where our minds jump from thought to thought without having a centralized idea to focus on. In the right circumstances when we want to escape our own realities for a moment, such as while running or cleaning your room, this practice of allowing your mind to wander off can be useful and can actually cleanse your mind and even bring up new insights to problems or obstacles that you might be facing. When it's time for us to hone in on the task at hand, we need to learn to be fully present and not let our minds wonder off into other frames of thought. With practice and repeatedly focusing on the one thing at hand you will begin to notice that this act of Hyper Focus and Attentiveness will be as simple as switching a light switch on or off.

As you go through this, focus solely on the words that you are reading. You can even imagine as if I'm standing right in front of you reading this section to you. Do your best to visualize the information that you are reading right now. Go ahead and relax your entire body. Let go of any stress that you might have in your mind and body. Envision a beam of blue relaxing light hovering above your head right now. Notice how the more that you focus on that beam of blue light, the more relaxed you feel. That's right. Notice how your heart rate is gently slowing down and matching your relaxed elongated brainwaves. As you see this beam of blue light gently enter your scalp and make its way through and around your brain, allow it to softly massage every lobe on your brain's right and left hemisphere. Notice how soothing this feels and now amplify the feeling of being relaxed as you see this blue beam of light make its way down your forehead, face, and neck area as it fully and gently relaxes every muscle that it comes in contact with.

Allow this relaxing beam of light to come down your shoulders, across your chest, down your arms, and through your fingertips. The soothing beam of light continues down your torso as it caresses your abdominal area. Notice that beam of light continue its way down your legs as it massages your thighs and down to the base of your calves. Allow the blue beam of relaxing light to every so softly swipe up the base of your foot and go through your toes as you now pay attention and notice your entire body feel very relaxed like a rag doll.

Notice a total sense of calmness rush your body as you are now at complete peace with everything that's around you and you can focus more intently on what's going on in the present moment.

In this state of mind, I want you to go ahead and let your creative imagination take over in a controlled manner. Imagine that you are at a horse race track and in the middle of the grassy field. The horses are already running circles around you along the sandy track. See them as they gallop round and round at an extremely fast pace. You can think of these horses as your thoughts. Each horse represents a new thought that our mind is trying to juggle throughout the day. Sometimes it might feel like we are not in full control of our thoughts, but know that you right now have the answer to being able to slow down and focus in on an individual thought or in this case a horse by making the other ones come to a halt for the time being.

Imagine that you have a pulley that controls the reigns of each one of these horses that are running around the track. Feel yourself gripping the pulley and tug on it ever so gently to see the immediate response that it has on all of the horses. Notice how each one of them starts to slow down. Now go ahead and tug on the pulley a little bit more. As you do that, that horses go from running to doing a nice calm lance around the track. In a controlled manner Pull on the reigns as you see the horses now come to a complete stop. Take a glance at each one of these horses. Because you have full control of their reigns, they are looking at you for the next command.

You point over to the horse's stables off to the left side of the tracks and let the horses know that they need to go over to their individual stall. One by one, each one of the horses gallops over to their own stall as you command the stalls to be shut closed.

You can let each of the horses out whenever you so pleased. If you want to just sit here in this warm grassy area and meditate while having a blank mind, you can do that as well.

Now as I count up from one to three, allow your mind to still be in a state of focus and relaxation while still being alert to your surroundings. One, notice some energy rising from the soles of your feet up your legs and thought your abdominal area. Two, allow that energy to come up your body as it wakes up your chest, arms, and shoulders. Three, notice this energy surrounding your entire body as you are now ready to Focus in on the next task at hand knowing that you have full control of your ability to control your thoughts just by thinking of that horse track metaphor.

Now that we're back, let's go into how to actually take the memory technique that we covered earlier and apply it to our everyday lives.

> Discipline is the bridge between goals and accomplishment.
> —Jim Rohn

SECTION III
MEMORY TRAINING

Chapter 8
More Locations = More Storage

"What about when we run out of locations when we need to memorize more information?"

That's the biggest concern that I get from individuals when they first learn this memory system. They fear that once they use up their first 10 locations, that they can't continue to use the system in order to memorize more information.

There are 2 solutions to this concern. The first one is to create more locations and the second one is to reuse the locations that we previously used in order to memorize more information. But then another question arises: "Wouldn't we get confused with what we memorized before and what we're trying to memorize now." If you haven't reviewed the old information plenty enough, then yes you will get interference. You must move that initial information that you stored on your locations into your long term memory and you do that by reviewing it several times over.

As memory athletes, we must not only master the art of memorizing information very quickly, but we must also become the masters of forgetting information. Since we're training to be able to go from memorizing a 100 digit number in 10 minutes to memorizing that same amount of digits in a matter of a few minutes, we must reuse the locations that we previously used for this memorization task. So how do we do it so that we don't mix up the old numbers that we previously memorized with the new numbers? As we have discussed already, we know that our brains tend to dissolute material that it doesn't deem important because it only saw it once, so we use a set of locations to memorize something then we don't reuse those locations again for a few days. We don't review the sequence of those numbers in that exact order past the initial point of recall.

Here is an example. If I have to memorize this 10 digit number as part of my training, 1234567890, I would see my images for that number interact with locations in my mom's house. Then I would only recall that number a few minutes after I had just memorized it, before moving on to my next trial run of a brand new set of numbers. For that next trial, I would go on to a new set of locations in my mom's house to memorize this sequence of random numbers: 0246813579. I would repeat this process again and again with new groups of locations until my training for that day wrapped up. Two or three days later, I would go back to the locations that were previously used and train in the numbers event once again. During that rest period the old images that I had stored along that route had already vanished or were at most extremely fuzzy images. The interference, if there was any, was very minimal and the strength of the newly created stories along that same route would overpower whatever residual visuals that I had before along that particular route.

I was at the supermarket recently, and the cashier looked at the face of the $50 bill that I gave him and made the following comment, "This is Grant." I immediately said, "yes. That's Ulysses S. Grant, the 18th President." He looked at me and was amazing at the fact that I knew that fact. Here's the thing, I was also shocked and amazed that I could recall that after over a year of not accessing this particular bit of information.

You see I had worked with my Bell High School students a year prior and helped them memorized the Presidents in order. We stored both of these along a set of locations that we created called the Universal City Locations. That's because I went around Universal City near Universal Studios in Hollywood, California and took pictures of all of the key places around that area. For the presidents, we pictured a washing machine on the glass doors of Game Stop in order to remember who the first president was. There are some game characters right above the doors, so we pictured an atomic bomb exploding up there in order to help us remember that the second president was Adams. We did this for all 44 presidents using 44 locations. The 18th location was a fencing area and we pictured a huge granite table top growing from that fence to help us remember that the 18th president was Ulysses S. Grant.

So when the cashier mentioned the name "Grant," my mind instantly jumped to that 18th location and saw the granite table top growing out of the fence. Once the visual is recalled, then all we have to do is translate it back into the actual information that it triggers, which in this case is the 18th President.

The kicker to all of this, is that I have reused those same Universal City locations to memorize hundreds of other things. I mainly use them to train for upcoming memory competitions. I've stored, numbers, words, and playing cards along that same route that I stored the presidents in. I've even stored the period table of elements along that same route. But because we reviewed the presidents in that same order so many times, it essentially became connected like a chain link and have locked on to one another. My brain moved it from short term memory into long term memory because it saw that it was important.

You see now that it is possible to memorize information on top of locations that you have previously used, but you must also focus your time on creating new journeys or mental maps in order to increase your storage size for the information that you want to memorize. Let's do that right now.

Just like how we created your first 10 locations by going through 2 rooms in your home, we're going to use that same method to create 10 more locations in your home. Go ahead and choose two more rooms for us to choose locations from. Remember to start at one point in your room, and go clockwise from that location. Here are my second two rooms in my home

MY SAMPLE LOCATIONS:

Kitchen	Bedroom
11. Plate Cabinet	16. Ceiling Fan
12. Sink	17. Closet
13. Toaster	18. Bed
14. Stove	19. Computer Desk
15. Fridge	20. Book Shelf

Your Next 10 Locations:

Room 3:	Room 4:
11. _____	16. _____
12. _____	17. _____
13. _____	18. _____
14. _____	19. _____
15. _____	20. _____

In order to make them stick to that order, you need to now review them. Go through this specific route forwards, backward, and by number. Quiz yourself by asking what was the location for number 14? What about location number 19? And the 11th location was? What about the 20th? I like to close my eyes and visualize myself walking through the new locations that I created and playing duck duck goose with them. You might want to try something like that out to embed this journey into your mind.

The next step that I do with the new locations that I just created, is use them to memorize information. This helps to further reinforce the new additions to my mental map. I'm going to give you 10 new things to memorize and we'll place them along room 3 and room 4 in your home. If you want to give it a shot on your own, go ahead and look at the list and visualize each thing on one location in that room. If you want me to help you create the stories along the route, I'll share my visuals with you after the list.

Memorize the Following 10 Things

1. Pencil
2. Swan
3. Tree
4. Floor
5. Hand
6. Sticks
7. Hook
8. Infinity Rings (∞)
9. The letter Q
10. Tent

Here's how I would picture these 10 things on my locations. I would see a pencil scribbling all over my first location in the 3rd room or location number 11 overall in my home. I would picture a swan hovering over my second location and pecking at it. The tree would be falling over on to my 3rd location and making a loud crashing sound. On my 4th location I would see myself picking up the floor and stacking it on top of that location. A hand would then be grabbing and squeezing the 5th spot in my 3rd room. Once I do 5, I then do a quick review. What was on location number 2? What about number 5? And how about number 1? Let' move on.

In my last room, I would picture sticks on fire on top of my 16th location or 1st location in this fourth room. The next one would see a pirate hook shredding to pieces that next location. The 18th location will have infinity rings (∞) being dropped on top of it. I would then see the letter Q going round and round on the 19th location. The 20th and final location will have myself pitching a tent and sleeping inside of it. Now what was on your 3rd location in this last room? What about the 1st location in room four? How about the 19th location, what did that one have?

Now go ahead and write down the 10 things that we memorized on the locations, from memory. Check your answers afterwards:

1. _____
2. _____
3. _____
4. _____
5. _____
6. _____
7. _____
8. _____
9. _____
10. _____

How did you do? Did you get them all right? If you did, awesome! If you didn't then the story between the item and the location needs to have some more interaction between the two. Do your best to add as many senses as possible. What do you see, hear, feel, taste, and smell on that location with the information that you want to memorize?

Remember these 10 things that we just memorized, because we're going to use them to learn how to count in a foreign language in a later chapter.

Creating new locations is an easy task to do. We can do it from wherever that we're at. I did a YouTube video where I demonstrated how you could create locations at the doctor's office. It's the same process as you did when we created a mental map journey in our home. I like to create chunks of 5 at a time. Depending on the place where I'm at, I can have 2-4 chunks of 5 locations.

My challenge for you now, is to create a new journey from a place that you've visited before or visit frequently. It could be the library, the store that you like to shop at, your car, it could be your place of work, your doctor's office, just chose a spot that you can see right now in your mind if you were to close your eyes. Look around this place and choose a few things that you can label as new locations.

For example, I was at Chipotle recently and I created a journey there. I chose the doors as location number 1, the menu holder as location number 2, the glass panel as number 3, the tortilla presser as loci #4, and the meats section as location number 5. I reviewed this a few times before proceeding to choose 5 more spots. Those were, the guacamole tray, the cash register, the chips section, the fridge, and the trash can area. Boom. I could have kept going with up to 10 more locations at this Chipotle.

Use the following section to write down 10-20 new locations

Name of Place: _____

1. _____
2. _____
3. _____
4. _____
5. _____

6. _____
7. _____
8. _____
9. _____
10. _____

11. _____
12. _____
13. _____
14. _____
15. _____

16. _____
17. _____
18. _____
19. _____
20. _____

Now you have up to 20 new locations to work with and to help you memorize more information. This is going to be very useful as we move forward with the rest of the book. Don't stop here though. Keep creating more locations using different places.

An assignment for you to practice right now would be to ask someone to give you a list of 10-20 things for you to memorize. Then use these newly created locations to memorize those 10-20 things.

Then let's continue with learning how to memorize names & faces.

> *Imagination is more important than knowledge.*
>
> —Albert Einstein

Chapter 9
Names and Faces

"Phillip?" you mentally say to yourself as you walk up to this individual that you met last week at an important meeting, "or was it Edgar?"

You're having a hard time recalling his name and you know that this isn't the first time that it has happened to you, so you greet him with the usual, "Hey **man**! How's it going?"

"Man", or "Bud", or even "Hey you" are the most common go to responses when our brain is kicking into overdrive trying to find their actual name but it ha s no luck at that point in time.

For the show Superhuman, I had to memorize over 500 pieces of information and got tested on it just a short time later that day. I had to memorize the First Names, Last Name Initials, City and State, and a Facial Features of the over 100 audience members in attendance. I managed to get my challenge 100% correct and thus helping me become the first ever Memory Master and Superhuman Champion!

Before I had the skills to be able to do what I did on the show, I was that person who would constantly forget someone else's name. It didn't even have to be an entire week or two before I forgot it. Many times it would be a few seconds after the person that I was having a conversation with gave me their name, that I would almost instantly forget it.

So if you're in that same boat, let me tell you right now that there is hope! I was able to turn my situation around after learning the memory techniques that I will be teaching you here and by practicing on a consistent basis. I know that once you go through this process and practice regularly with every person that you meet or have met, then you will become a master at remembering names!

Whether an individual wants to compete in a memory competition, or is someone who wants to excel in their career field, How to Remember Names and Faces, is the number 1 most requested topic that I get from those people wanting to improve their memory. It was requested so much that as I was starting to write this book, I focused a huge portion of my time in this chapter that I decided to create a book dedicated to just names. It is still a Number 1 Best Selling Book right now. It's called, you guessed it, "How to Remember Names and Faces."

I'm going to give you several examples here as to how you can apply the memorization technique to being able to memorize anyone's name.

The Key to Memorizing Names

As you know, the key to memorization is visualization. In order to remember a name, we need to turn that name into an image. We then have to create a story to link that name to the person somehow.

When I perform my Better Memory Now for Professionals Workshop, I start off by recalling the names of all of the individuals that I met earlier that day. How I do this is as I'm walking to someone I pay attention to facial features or even clothing that stands out. If the person that I'm walking up to has a bushy beard, I will make a mental note of that and then go about exchanging names. If he says that his name is Albert, I will quickly visualize an Owl eating a Burrito on his beard. Albert = Owl + Burrito. I might review that image once or twice very quickly as we talk for a few moments. Just take a quick glance to his beard and see the Owl and Burrito. Then when it comes time to recall his name later on in the afternoon, I will look at that beard, see the story that I created, and say "and you are Albert!"

Another tip is to ask yourself not only what does this name remind me of but also who does this name remind me. Do you know of someone else with that same name? If you do, you can add that person to the story. I have a brother law named Albert, so I will picture my brother in law interacting with this person named Albert. Maybe they're both eating burritos with an Owl. The stranger and quirkier the story, the easier that it is for you to recall it later on.

Let me give you another example here.

Imagine that you are walking up to this young lady.

She tells you that her name is Julia and you quickly picture Jewels.

I want you to associate those Jewels doing something on Julia.

Perhaps the Jewels are sliding down her hair like a water slide as they yell out, "JUUUULLLLIIIIAAAA"

Make the image vivid. Add as many senses as you can to bring the story to life. What do you hear, what do you see, are there any smells, tastes, feelings that arise? Remember that the more graphic the story, the more links that you are creating in your brain to tell it that this person is important and that it should hold on to their name for a longer period of time.

More Names

That was pretty easy and fun, right?
Now let's create some more pictures for common names.

Angela = Angel
Bill = Bill Clinton or Dollar Bill
Chris = Cross
Frank = Franks sausage
Jacky = Car Jack
Jennifer = Chimney + Fur
Lisa = Lisa Simpson
Luis = Lace
Sandra = Sand
Rosa = Rose
Vince = Fence
Zach = Potato Sack

With those done, let's attach them to some faces.
I want you take your time and have these pictures interact with each individual. Make sure to review them to cement them into your mind after each row.

Then see how many you can get correct.

QUIZ YOURSELF WITH THE FOLLOWING FACES

Better Memory Now

70

ANSWERS ON THE NEXT PAGE

Answers:

1. Angela
2. Bill
3. Chris
4. Frank
5. Jacky
6. Jennifer
7. Lisa
8. Luis
9. Sandra
10. Rosa
11. Vince
12. Zach

How did you do?

Now if you do this for every person that you meet, I guarantee that you will see an improvement in your ability to retain the names of all of those people.

A tip that I can give you to help strengthen this memory process of remembering names, is to use the association that you have for the person's name as a conversation starter. Not only will it help you with breaking the ice, but it will help you to anchor in their name on a deeper level. Many times, when it is appropriate to do so and I know that the image won't offend the individual, the following scenario will happen:

Me: "Hi my name is Luis Angel, what's your name?"
Person: "Nice to meet you, I'm Michael."
Me: "Dude, Michael Jackson is one of my favorite all time entertainers!"
Michael: "Haha… Really? Mine too! Billy Jean is my favorite song…"

And the conversation continues.

What happens here is that you're linking something that you have a strong connection to in your mind, in this case Michael Jackson, with the individual that you are meeting and you will have a better chance of remembering that person's name later on. Use this technique. It works!

For long term memory retention, I highly recommend that you keep a notebook or some type of online document where you can jot down the names and some of the characteristics of the people that you meet throughout the day. This is what I do. At the end of each day, I open up a spreadsheet where I quickly write down the names of all the people that I met and what stood out to me about those individuals. So if I met Ashley with Long Wavy Dark Hair at the grocery store, that's exactly what I would write down. I week later, I take a minute or two to review all of the people that I met that week or two prior.

This reinforces those stories and pictures that you linked to those individuals, so that if you bump into them a month later at the store, you will be able to say, "Hey Ashley! It's great to see you again."

I will include a full list of the images that I use for every person that I meet in the following pages.

Better Memory Now

MALE NAMES

Aaden	A Den with Apple	Archer	Bow and Arrow
Aarav	A Ref (referee)	Archie	Archery
Aaron	Air Gun	Ariel	Mermaid
Abdiel	Ape Dealing Cards	Armand	Arm Band
Abdullah	Ape Doll saying ah	Armando	A Mango
Abel	A Pill	Arnold	Arm Hold
Abraham	A Bra with Ham	Art	Art Work
Abram	A Broom	Arthur	Arthur Cartoon
Ace	Ace Card	Arturo	A Turtle
Adam	Atom	Ashton	Ton of Ashes
Adan	Apple Don (mob)	Atticus	Attic
Aden	A Den	August	A Gust
Adrian	A drain	Austin	Cowboy Boot (Texas)
Adriel	A drill	Avery	Ivory Tooth
Agustin	A Gust Tin Can	Axel	Ax
Ajay	A Jay (Jordan Shoe)	Barney	Barney
Al	Owl	Barrett	Rat in a Bar
Alan	Alan Wrench	Barry	Berry
Albert	Burnt Owl	Bart	Bart Simpson
Alberto	Burnt Toe	Bautista	Boat Taking Test
Alec	A Lick	Beckett	Bucket
Alejandro	Owl Hands Drying	Ben	Bench
Alessandro	A lasso in sand	Benjamin	Bench Jam
Alex	Owl that Licks	Bennett	Bent Net
Alexander	Owl Sander	Benny	Bending
Alexzander	Licking a Sander	Benson	Bending Sun
Alfonso	Owl Phone	Bently	Bentley Car
Alfred	Owl Fried	Bernard	St Bernard Dog
Ali	Muhammad Ali	Bernie	Burning Knee
Alonso	A Lasso	Bert	Bird
Alonzo	A Lasso Zebra	Bill	Duck's Bill
Alvin	Alvin (chipmunk)	Billy	Billy goat
Amare	A Mare	Blake	Bake Blade
Amir	A mirror	Bo	Bow Tie
Amos	A Moth	Bob	Bobsled
Andre	Hand Dry	Bobby	Bobby Pin
Andres	Ant wearing Dress	Boston	Ton of Busts
Andrew	Ants Drew	Brad	Bread
Andy	Ants Drinking Tea	Bradford	Bread in a Ford
Angel	Angel	Bradley	Bread with Leaves
Angelo	angel eating Jell-O	Brady	Braided hair
Anthony	ants in a tree	Brandon	Branded
Anton	Ton of Ants	Brendan	Braid Hen
Apollo	A stick (palo)	Brent	Brown Tent

MALE NAMES

Brett	Brat	Cliff	Cliff
Brian	Brain	Clifford	Clifford Dog
Brock	Brown Rock	Clint	Tint
Broderick	Brown Brick	Clinton	Ton of Lint
Bruce	Prune Juice	Clyde	Clydesdale horse
Bruno	Brown Nose	Cody	Code
Bud	Rose Bud	Colby	Cold Bee
Byron	Bicycle Running	Cole	Coal
Cameron	Camera	Coleman	Coleman Grill
Camilo	Camel Lost	Colin	Calling
Camron	Camel Running	Collin	Calling
Cannon	Cannon	Colt	Colt (Baby Horse)
Carl	Curl	Conner	Can of Nar
Carlos	Car Lace	Connor	Can of Nar
Carlton	Carton (Milk)	Conrad	Convict Rat
Carmelo	Caramel	Cooper	Chicken Coop
Carson	Car Son (little boy)	Corey	Apple Core
Carter	Charter a Boat	Cory	Apple Core
Cary	Carry	Craig	Crate
Case	Case (Briefcase)	Cristian	Christ
Casen	Case Net	Crosby	Crowbar
Casey	Case Yoyo	Cruz	Cruz Azul
Cash	Cash (ATM)	Curis	Curry Soup
Cason	Cat Gas On	Curt	Curtain
Ceasar	Julius Caesar	Curtis	Curtains Snake
Cecil	Seal	Dan	Dam
Cedric	Red Brick	Daniel	Downey (laundry)
Chad	ChapStick	Danny	Danish
Chance	Chance game	Dante	Diente (tooth with sombrero)
Chandler	Chandelier	Darrell	Barrel
Charles	Charcoal	Darren	Dart Run
Charlie	Charcoal Leaves	Darryl	Dog Barrel
Chase	Chase Credit Card	Dave	Cave
Chava	Guava	David	Bladed
Chester	Chest Drawers	Deacon	Bacon with D
Chet	Cheese Jet	Deandre	Tea Latte
Chris	Cross	Dennis	Dentist
Christian	Christ on Cross	Denzel	Denzel Washington
Christopher	Cross Gopher	Derek	Deer Brick
Chuck	Chalk	Derrick	Deer Brick
Clark	Clock	Dexter	Dexter's Laboratory
Claude	Cloud	Dick	Deck
Clay	Clay	Diego	Diego (Dora's)
Clayton	Ton of Clay	Dion	The On (light switch)

MALE NAMES

Dirk	Dirt	Fisher	Fisherman
Dominic	Dome Picnic	Fletcher	Fetcher
Dominick	Dominoes	Floyd	Flood
Don	Don	Francisco	Frank Sausage on Disco
Donald	Donald Duck	Franco	Frank Sausage O
Donovan	Dino Van	Frank	Frank Sausage
Doug	Dig	Frankie	Frank Sausage Envelope
Douglas	Dug a Glass	Franklin	Franklin Turtle
Drake	Drake rapper	Fred	Fried Egg
Drew	Drew	Freddy	Freddy Krueger
Duane	Drain	Frederick	Fried Brick
Dunking	Dunking	Gabriel	Gabble
Dustin	Dusting	Gael	Gargoyle
Dusty	Dust Powder	Gage	Gauge
Dwayne	The Rock	Garrett	Carrot
Dwight	White Dog	Gary	Garage
Dylan	Dill Pickle Ant	Geoffrey	Chef in a Tree
Earl	Pearl	George	Curious George
Ed	Head	Gerald	Chair that is Old
Eddie	Yeti	Gil	Fish Gil
Edgar	Head Gear	Gilbert	Gil Bird
Edmund	Head Mount	Giovanni	Cheeto Van Eye
Eduardo	Head Door	Giovanny	Cheeto Van
Edward	Head Wired	Glenn	Gluing
Edwin	Head and Wind	Gordon	Gordo (chubby)
Eli	Eel in Eye	Graham	Graham Crackers
Elon	Elephant Long	Grant	Granite (rock)
Emiliano	M&M Lion	Greg	Keg
Emilio	M&M Bolio (bread)	Guillermo	Guile vs Elmo
Emmanuel	Elephant manual	Gus	Gust of Wind
Emmitt	A Mitt	Gustavo	Gust Towel
Eric	Ear Ache	Hal	Hail
Erick	Ear Ache Kangaroo	Hank	Handkerchief
Ernesto	Ear Nest	Hans	Hands
Ernie	Ear and Knee	Harold	Old Hair
Erwin	Ear and Wind	Harry	Hair
Esteban	A Star in Van	Hector	Heckler
Ethan	Eating	Henry	Hen Rowing
Evan	Oven	Herb	Herb
Everette	Sever It	Herbert	Herb and Bird
Feibi	Frisbee	Homer	Homer Simpson
Felipe	Flip Elephant	Houston	Houston Rocket
Felix	Felix the Cat	Howard	How Indian
Fernando	Fern Ant	Hugh	Ewe

Memory Training

MALE NAMES

Name	Association	Name	Association
Hugo	Juice	Jon	Toilet
Hunter	Hunter	Jonah	Whale
Ian	Indian	Jonas	Jelly Donuts
Ignacio	Igloo Nacho	Jonathan	Toilet is Thin
Iman	Magnet (Spanish)	Jonathon	Toilet is Thin
Irv	Nerve	Jordan	Michael Jordan
Irving	Swerving	Jorge	Curious George juice
Isaac	Eye Sack	Jose	Hose (water)
Isayas	Ice Age	Joseph	Sloppy Joe on Sofa
Ismael	He's Smiling	Joshua	Shower
Ivan	Eye on Van	Josue	Shower Elephant
Jack	Car Jack	Juan	Wand
Jake	Cake	Jud	Jug
Jackson	Michael Jackson	Jude	Food
Jacob	Cake Cob (corn)	Julian	Jewel on Ant
Jaden	Skating J's (Jordan shoes)	Julio	Jewel Hanging
Jaime	Jamaica (Hibiscus tea)	Junior	June Bug
Jake	Shade	Justin	Just Do It Woosh
Jameer	Jam Deer	Keith	Keys
James	chains	Ken	Can
Jared	Chair Red	Kendrick	Can Brick
Jason	Jaybird in Sun	Kenneth	Can and Net
Javier	Javon (soap) Tire	Kent	Tent
Jay	Jaybird	Keshawn	Key Shine
Jeff	Chef in a Tree	Kevin	Cave Oven
Jeffrey	Geoffrey Giraffe	Kirk	Kick
Jeremiah	Cherry Jemima (syrup)	Klay	Clay Kangaroo
Jeremy	Cherry Mime	Kobe	Kobe Bryant
Jerimiah	Cherry Jemima (syrup) Ice	Kurt	Cut Curtain
Jerome	Chair Roam	Kyle	Tile
Jeronimo	Chair Dominoes	Lamar	Lace Mare
Jerry	Cherry	Lance	Sir Lancelot
Jess	Chest	Landry	Laundry
Jesse	Cheesy	Larry	Lariat
Jesus	Jesus	Lautaro	El Torro (the bull)
Jett	Jet	Lawrence	Law for Ants
Jim	Gym	Lebron	Lead brown
Jionni	Chonies (underwear)	Lee	Leaves
Joaquin	Joking Clown	Lemond	Lemon
Joe	Sloppy Joe Hamburger	Len	Lens
Joel	Jewel	Leo	Lion
Joey	Kangaroo	Leon	Lean On
John	Toilet	Leonardo	Lion with Nar (pomegranate)
Johnny	Chonies with Yoyo	Leroy	Lens in Toy

MALE NAMES

Les	Less Than Sign <	Morris	Morris The Cat
Levi	Levi Pants	Moses	Mud Roses
Lincoln	Lincoln	Nate	Nap Gate
Lionel	Lionel train	Nathan	Gnat
Livan	Levis Van	Neal	Nail
Lloyd	Lid	Ned	Ned Flanders
Lou	Blue	Nelson	Nail Sun
Lucas	Lucas Candy	Nick	Nickel
Luciano	I Love Lucy Ants	Nicolas	Nickel Gas
Luis	Lace	Nikola	Nikola Tesla
Luke	Luke Warm Water	Noah	No Air
Luther	Devil	Noel	Christmas Noel
Lyle	Aisle	Norman	Norseman
Mack	Mack Truck	Oliver	Olive
Manny	Man with Money	Omid	Ham Mud
Manuel	Manuel Book	Oscar	Academy award
Marcos	Markers with Snake	Otis	Otis Elevator
Marcus	Mucus	Owen	Owing
Mario	Super Mario	Pablo	Popsicle
Mark	Marker	Pat	Pat Something
Marlon	Marlin Nemo	Patricio	Patting Rice
Marshall	Law Enforcement	Patrick	St Patrick
Martin	Martian	Paul	Ball
Marvin	Carving	Pedro	Paid to Row
Mason	Mason Jar	Pete	Pete Moss
Mateo	Mat Boxeo	Peter	Peter cottontail
Matias	Mat Dice	Phil	Fill Up
Matt	Door Mat	Pierre	Pier
Matthew	Matt in a Pew	Preston	Pressing a Ton
Maurice	More Rice	Quincy	Wind and Sea
Mauricio	More Rice in O	Rafael	Roof Owl
Max	Mix	Rajon	Rat Toilet
Maximiliano	Mixing Mime Lion	Ralph	Raft
Maximo	Mix Mole	Ramiro	Ram with Mirror
Maxwell	Mix Well	Ramon	Ramon Noodles
Mel	Melon	Randal	Ran Doll
Melvin	Melt Van	Randall	Ran Doll Laser
Michael	Bicycle	Randolph	Ram with Dolphin
Mickey	Mickey Mouse	Randy	Ran Dice
Miguel	My Goal (soccer)	Ray	Ray of Light
Mike	Microphone	Raymond	Ray on a Mound
Miles	Miles	Reggie	Wrench Squeegee
Mitch	Mitt	Rex	T-Rex
Morgan	Organ	Ricardo	Recorder

MALE NAMES

Name	Mnemonic	Name	Mnemonic
Richard	Rich Yard	Sid	Sit
Richie	Dollar Sign	Simon	Simon Game
Rick	Brick	Spencer	Dispenser
Rob	Robber	Stan	A Stan
Robbie	Robe	Steve	Stove
Robert	Robot	Steven	Stove Oven
Rod	Rod	Stewart	Steward
Roderick	Rod in a Brick	Stu	Stew
Rodney	Rod in Knee	Sylvester	Sylvester Cat
Rodrigo	Rod Rug	Tad	Tadpole
Rogelio	Row of Jell-O	Tansel	Utensil
Roger	Rod in Chair	Ted	Ted Bear Dead
Roland	Rolling	Teddy	Teddy Bear
Roman	Roman Soldier	Terry	Tearing an Envelope
Ron	Rabbit Run	Tex	Texas
Ronald	Ronald McDonald	Theodore	Teeth on Door
Ronnie	Running	Thomas	Thermos
Ross	Boss	Tim	Tin Can
Rowan	Rowing	Timothy	Tin of Tea
Roy	Roy Rogers	Toby	Toe and Bee
Ruben	Ruben Sandwich	Todd	Toad
Rudolph	Rudolph Red Nose	Tom	Tom Cat
Russ	Rusts	Tomas	Dome with snakes
Russell	Rustle	Tommy	Tommy gun
Ryan	Sea Lion	Tony	Tony the Tiger
Ryder	Bike Rider	Tracy	Tracing with Stencil
Sam	Uncle Sam	Trevor	Tree Beaver
Sammy	Uncle Sam on knee	Troy	Troy Movie
Samuel	Uncle Sam on mule	Ty	Tie
Sandy	Sand	Tyler	Tire
Santiago	Saint Eating Eggo	Tyrese	Tie Rose
Santino	Saint on Dinosaur	Tyrone	Tie Rowing
Santos	Multiple Saints	Tyson	Mike Tyson
Saul	Salt	Valentino	Valentine Card
Scott	Scott paper towels	Van	Van
Sean	Shark Yawning Envelope	Vern	Fern
Sebastian	Sebastian the Crab	Vernon	Furry Nun
Sergio	Surge Protector	Vic	Vick's cough drop
Seymour	See More	Vicente	Fence with Sombrero
Shane	Shine	Victor	Flick Door
Shawn	Shark Yawning	Vince	Fence
Sheldon	Shielding	Vincent	Fencing
Sherman	German Shepard	Wade	Wade in Pool
Sid	Sit	Wallace	Walrus

MALE NAMES

Walter	Cup of Water
Ward	Wart
Warren	Warden
Wayne	Rain
Willie	Free Willy Whale
Winston	Wind Ton

FEMALE NAMES

Name	Association	Name	Association
Aaliyah	Owl Idea (light Bulb)	Audrey	Laundry
Abby	A Bee	Autumn	Leaves
Abigail	A bee in a pail	Barbara	Barbed Wire
Ada	A Doll	Beatrice	Beat Rice
Adell	A Bell	Becky	Horse Bucking
Adriana	A Drain	Belinda	Bee Lint
Agustina	A Gust	Bernadette	Burn a Net
Alejandra	Owl Hands Drying	Bernice	Burn Dice (on fire)
Alessandra	A Lasso in Sand	Bessie	Beso (kiss)
Alice	Lice	Beth	Bath
Alicia	Owl Shield	Bethany	Bath Tub Knee
Alise	Owl Shoelace	Betty	Betting
Allison	Lice in the sun	Beverly	Bed of Leaves
Allysa	A Lasso	Bianca	Binaca (mouth spray)
Allyson	A Lice Sun yoyo	Billie	Billy Goat
Alma	Owl mom	Blanca	White
Alondra	A Laundry	Bobbie	Fishing Bobber
Amanda	A Man and Dog	Bonnie	Bonnet
Amber	Flame	Brenda	Brand New Dog
Amelia	Email (envelope)	Briana	Brain
Amy	Aiming	Bridget	Bridges
Ana	Ant Apple	Britney	Britney Spears
Andrea	Ant Drinking Water	Brooklyn	Brakes
Angel	Angel	Camila	Camel Lace
Angela	Jell-O	Camille	Camel
Angelica	Angel Cuffs	Candice	Can of Dice
Angelina	Angelina Jolie	Candy	Candy
Angie	Algae	Carla	Car with Lace
Anilette	A Knee Lid	Carmen	Car and Man
Anita	Kneading	Carol	Carol
Ann	Ant	Carol	Christmas Carol
Annabelle	Ant Bell	Carolina	Carolina Panther
Annette	A Net	Carolyn	Caroling Lint
Annie	Orphan Annie	Carrie	Carry
Antonia	Ant Toe Nail	Catalina	Catalina Island
April	A Pill	Catherine	Cat Running
Ariana	Ariana Grande	Celeste	Cell Phone Stars
Ariel	Mermaid	Celia	Cell Phone
Arlene	Ark Lean	Charlotte	Spider Web
Ashley	Ashes	Chelsea	Shell See
Ashlyn	Ash Violin	Cheryl	Chair that is Ill
Astrid	Ostrich	Chloe	Clover
Athena	Athena Goddess	Chris	Cross
Aubrey	I Breath(elizer)	Chrissy	Cross in the Sea

FEMALE NAMES

Christine	Christmas tree	Faith	Church
Cristine	Cross in Stone	Fatima	Fat Mouse
Cicely	Sister Silly	Felicia	Fleece
Cindy	Cinnamon Candy	Fernanda	Fern Ant
Claire	Clear Eyes	Florence	Flour Rinse
Clara	Clarinet	Frances	Eiffel Tower
Claudia	Cloud	Gabriela	Gable Roof
Colleen	Calling	Gabrielle	Gabrielle Olympics
Connie	Convict	Gaby	Cabbie
Crystal	Crystal Vase	Gail	Gale Force Winds
Cynthia	Cinder Block	Genece	Jean Knees
Dakota	Duck Coat	Genesis	Jean Sister
Daniela	Downey Lace	Georgia	Gorge
Daphne	Dolphin	Gina	Greener
Darlene	Door with Beans	Ginger	Ginger Bread Man
Dawn	Dawn	Ginny	Bottle of Gin on Knees
Debbie	Dead Bee	Giselle	Chisel
Deborah	Dead Boar	Giuliana	Glue
Debra	Deer Zebra	Glenda	Blender
Delanda	Dell Comp. on Land	Gloria	Old Glory
Denise	Disease	Grace	Saying a Prayer
Desiree	Dessert	Gris	Grease oil
Destiny	Desk Tiny	Guadalupe	Guacamole Loop
Diana	Dying Ants	Hannah	Hand
Dixie	Confederate Flag	Harper	Harp
Donna	Donald Duck	Harriet	Lariat
Doris	Doors	Hattie	Hat
Dorothy	Door Teeth	Hazel	Hazelnut Ice-cream
Dottie	Dots	Heather	Feather
Edna	Head Nut	Heaven	Oven
Eileen	Eye Leaning	Heidi	Hiding
Elaine	Airplane	Helen	Halo Melon
Eleanor	Plane Landing on Door	Hilda	Hold Apple
Elise	A Lease	Holly	Boughs of Holly
Elizabeth	Lizard Breath	Hope	Hop over Rope
Ellen	Island	Ida	Idaho Potato
Ellie	Smelly	Irene	Eye Ring
Emily	Family	Iris	A Wrist
Emma	Email	Irma	Ear Muff
Erica	Ear	Isabel	Ice Bell
Erin	Earing	Isabelle	Ice Bell Lion
Eva	Evil (horns)	Ivy	Poison Ivy
Eve	Eve Paws	Jackie	Car Jack
Evelyn	Violin	Jacqueline	Lint on a Jack

FEMALE NAMES

Jade	Jade stone	Laura	Laurels
Jamie	Chain on Knees	Lauren	Laurel Run
Jan	Jam	Laurie	Lowering Crane
Jane	Jane Tarzan	Layla	Lay Down
Janet	Jam in a Net	Leslie	Less than Sign <
Janice	Jam Ice	Lexi	Flexing
Jazmin	Jasmine Princess	Lillian	Lily with Ants
Jean	Jeans	Lily	Lily flower
Jeanette	Jeans in a Net	Linda	Lion Dog Leash
Jeanie	Genie	Lindsey	Lint See
Jennifer	Chin Fur	Lisa	Mona Lisa
Jenny	Chimney	Liz	Lizard
Jessica	Chest with Cuffs	Lois	Lace
Jill	Pill	Lola	Lollipop
Jo	Sloppy Joe Burger	Loretta	Lobo Beretta
Joan	Joan of Arc	Lori	Loar Guitar
Joanne	Sloppy Joe w/ ants	Lorraine	Low Rain
Jocelyn	Chest Lint	Louise	Low Easel
Joy	Joy dishwashing liquid	Luana	Luna (moon) apple
Joyce	Juice	Lucille	Loose Sail
Juanita	One Knee	Lucinda	Loose Rope on Cinder Block
Judith	Chew Desk	Lucy	I Love Lucy
Judy	Judge Judy	Luna	Luna (moon)
Julia	Jewel Apple	Lupe	Loop (earing)
Juliana	Jewel Ant Apple	Lydia	Lid
Julie	Jewelry	Lynn	Lint
Juliet	Jewel Net	Madeline	Mad at Lint
June	June Bug	Mae	Mayo
Kaitlyn	Kite LInt	Maggie	Maggie's Pacifier (Simpsons)
Karen	Carrot	Mandy	Mandolin
Kassandra	Case Sand	Marcy	Marching
Kate	Gate	Margaret	Market
Katherine	Cat that Runs	Margarita	Margarita Drink
Kathleen	Cat that Leans	Marge	Marge Simpson Hair
Kathy	Cat Teeth	Maria	Sangria Wine
Katie	Kite	Marian	Mare with Ants
Kay	Key	Marianne	Marry Ant
Kelly	Surfboard (Kelly Slater)	Marie	Mare
Kendra	Can Draw	Marilyn	Marry Lint
Khloe	Clover (Kangaroo)	Marina	Marry Run
Kim	Climb	Marissa	Marry Seesaw
Kimberly	Swim Bear	Marjorie	My Jury
Kirsten	Skirt Stem	Marlene	Mare Lean
Latoya	Lace on Toy	Marry Ellen	Marry a Melon

FEMALE NAMES

Marsha	Marshmallow	Peg	Peg
Martha	Vineyard	Peggy	Peg Yoyo
Mary	Merry Go Round	Penny	Penny Coin
Megan	Mayo Bacon	Phyllis	Philly
Melanie	Melon on Knee	Priscilla	Pass the Jell-O
Melissa	Molasses	Rachel	Ray Shining on a Shell
Meredith	Mare in a Dish	Ramona	Ram Moaning
Michelle	Shell Sleeping (mimi)	Rebecca	Rope Deck
Mikayla	Milk Laugh	Renee	Raining Elephants
Mila	Miel (Honey)	Roberta	Robot
Minnie	Minnie Mouse	Robin	Bird
Miriam	Mirror Ham	Rochelle	Rowing Shells
Mitzi	Mitt that can See	Rocio	Rice O
Molly	Mole	Rosa	Rose (Red)
Mona	Moaning	Rosalie	Rose Leaves (Pedals)
Monica	Harmonica	Rosalyn	Rose Lint
Monique	Money Kangaroo	Rose	Rose (White)
Morgan	Organ	Rosie	Rosie Blush
Mya	Mime Apple	Roxanne	Rocks in Hand
Nan	Nun	Ruth	Baby Ruth candy bar
Nancy	Nun Eating Seeds	Sadie	Saddle
Naomi	Knight Mime	Sally	Salad
Natalia	Net Telly (TV) w/ Apple	Samantha	Saw man
Natalie	Net Telly (TV)	Sandra	Sander
Nellie	Kneeling	Sandy	Sand
Nicole	Nickel	Sarah	Sarah Lee cup cakes
Nina	Knee	Sasha	Sash
Nirey	Knee Crown (rey)	Scarlett	Scar Lid
Nora	Snoring	Selena	Selling Cash Register
Noreen	No Rain	Serena	Tennis Racket (Williams)
Norma	Normal (gauge)	Sharon	Sharing
Olive	Olives	Sheila	Shield
Olivia	Oh Liver!	Shelley	Shells
Paige	Page (paper)	Sherry	Bottle of Sherry
Pam	Spam	Sheryl	Shirt that is Ill
Pamela	Paneling	Shirley	Shirt Sleeves
Paris	Parrot	Sidney	Sit on Knee
Pat	Act of Patting	Sky	Blue Sky
Patricia	Pats of Butter	Sofia	Sofa
Patty	Hamburger Patty	Sonia	Sony Walkman
Paula	Polo	Sophia	Sew a Bee
Paulina	Pole Leaning on Apple	Stacy	Stacy Adams Shoes
Pauline	Pole that Leans	Stephanie	Step on Knees
Pearl	Pearl	Sue	Suit

FEMALE NAMES

Sue Ann	Suit with Ants	Velma	Velma Glasses
Summer	Hot Sun	Veronica	Violin Harmonica
Susan	Lazy Susan	Vicky	Vick's cough drops
Susannah	Snoozing hand	Victoria	Victory Trophy
Susie	Snoozing	Viki	Vicks Vaporub
Suzanne	Snoozing Ant	Virginia	Fur Genie
Sylvia	Silverware	Vivian	Bib on Van
Tammy	Tummy	Wanda	Wand
Tanya	Tan Yoyo	Wendy	Wendy's Pigtails
Teresa	Tree Saw	Wilma	Wilma Flintstone
Terry	Terry Cloth	Windy	Wind
Tess	Test	Yesenia	Yellow Sony CD player
Tracy	Tracing Stencil	Yvette	Corvette
Valentina	Valentine Card	Yvonne	Eve Van (dog van)
Valeria	Valet Guy	Zoe	Sewing
Valerie	Library	Zoey	Zoo animals
Vanessa	van wearing a dress		

In my book, "How to Remember Names and Faces," I have over 500 examples of faces and names for you to practice with. I would highly recommend that book to you if you want to truly become a master at remembering names.

Bonus: Social Interactions

"Hi Jeff, how was the ski trip that you were planning on taking last month? Did Carol and the kids have fun going down the slopes? I know that little Jimmy was really excited to see snow for the first time."

Being able to remember things about the people that you meet, is very important when it comes to building relationships especially if you are attempting to do business with them in some capacity. The huge issue that I had in the past was that I would talk to someone about something important to them, and during the next interaction that we would have a few weeks later, I would totally fail to bring up anything from the previous conversation because I forgot what we had talked about. If this has ever happened to you before, let me give you my tips on how to not let this happen in the future.

As with everything else that we want to remember for a longer period of time, we need to visualize the information that we want to remember. So the first thing that I would do is transform the gentleman's name into an image. Jeff equals chef. He then proceeded to tell me about a ski trip that he was going to take with his family. As he would be telling me this, I would pretend like there was a huge movie screen in front of me and I was playing out the information on that screen and Jeff was the narrator. On the screen, I would see Jeff with a chef hat skiing down a snowy mountain. He told me that his wife Carol and Jimmy had never been to the snow before, so I would picture a lady singing Christmas Carols with a boy eating Slim Jim as they roll around the snow for the 1st time.

The next step here is to review. Like I explained earlier, when I meet someone new I like to write down their names on an excel spreadsheet. Next to that line with their names, I'll also write down a few key things that we talked about. What I will also do, is the next day as I'm working out, driving, or just going about my day, I'll do a passive review. Meaning I'll picture the people that I met the previous day while doing those other activities and visualize the things that we talked about. Do this and it will help you to recall that information easier the next time that you see that person.

> Imagination is more important than knowledge.
>
> —Albert Einstein

Chapter 10
Numbers – The Basics

A floor tile smacks a bone which gets stuck on a jail cell that is full of mail envelopes with footballs inside of them.

Weird story, I know. But what you just did if you managed to clearly picture that visual in your mind, is memorize the following sequence of numbers: 3.141592653589.

This shouldn't come as a shocker to you that we created a weird story in order to memorize the first few digits of pi. You already know that the secret to memorization is visualization and that's no different when we want to memorize a random number. At the world memory championship, I was able to memorize a 120 digit number in 5 minutes using this method of storytelling.

I normally open my school Better Memory Now presentations with this demonstration. I tell the kids to write down a 50 digit number on the board. I look at it really quickly and then turn my back to the board, close my eyes, start waving my hands in the air as I recite every single digit. At the end of my entire workshop, I recite the entire 50 digit number backwards!

With a little bit of training and practice, you too will be able to memorize a long number in a matter of minutes and be able to recite it forwards and backwards.

The first thing that we have to do is associate images for every number between 00 and 99. That way as soon as we see or hear a number, we'll instantly have a predetermined image associated to that number and we can memorize it much more quickly. In the above example, 15 = Tile, 92 = Bone, 65 = Jail, 35 = Mail, and 89 = Football.

At the beginning of this book I actually gave you the first 10 images for the single digits. 1 = Hat, 2 = Honey, 3 = Ham, 4 = Hour Glass, 5 = Hail, 6 = Hash brown, 7 = Hook, 8 = Hoof, 9 = Hoop, 0 = House.

"Mister, I noticed that all of these things start with the letter 'H'."

That's correct. The reason for this is that every number between 00-99 has two digits, and the way this system works is that you need a certain sound associated with each number in order to create a picture. For single digits, since there is only one number we have to add a filler sound in front in order to create the image.

Here are the consonant sounds that each number has:

1 = T, D, Th
2 = N
3 = M
4 = R
5 = L
6 = J, Sh, Ch, g (soft)
7 = C (hard), K, Ck, G (hard)
8 = F, V
9 = B, P
0 = S, c (soft), Z

Instead of trying to memorize these sounds with brute force, I'm going to teach you how to do it the way that my mentor, Ron White taught me. We are going to create body locations. As we go through them, make sure to use the exact same label that is given for each body location.

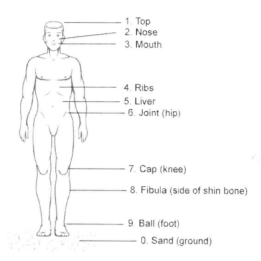

The Top of our head will be location number 1 and it will just be called "Top." Our second body location is Nose, number 3 is Mouth, number 4 is Ribs, and our fifth location is Liver. Now review. Say these first 5 locations forwards, backwards, and by number. What was location number 2? What about the first one? And how about the 5th location? Great! Now let's move on to the next 5.

The 6th location is your hip joint, but we're just going to call it "Joint." The seventh location is your knee cap, and we'll call this location "Cap." The eight location is your fibula bone which is the bone that runs up and down the side of your shin. The 9th location is the ball of your foot, and we'll call this "Ball." This last one is technically the tenth location, but per this system it is considered location number 0 and we'll picture Sand on the ground. Location zero is "Sand." Now go ahead and do a review with these last 5 body locations. Once you're done with that review all 10 of the body locations going forwards, backwards, and by number.

Body Locations

1 = Top
2 = Nose
3 = Mouth
4 = Ribs
5 = Liver
6 = Joint (hip)
7 = Cap (knee)
8 = Fibula
9 = Ball (foot)
0 = Sand (ground)

We use the first letter of each body location to remember the sound associated to each number. If the number is 22, you know that the sounds associated to these number are "N" and "N". You then throw in a few vowels to get an image out of it. My picture for 22 is Neon sign. Possibly picture an "OPEN" Neon sign for the number 22.

If I give you the number "40" and tell you to come up with an image for it, what would you picture? The first thing that you want to do is sound it out. You already know that the "4" has an "R" sound and the "0" has an "S" sound, so you have R_ S_ as your main triggers. Now throw in some vowels to come up with the actual image. My picture for 40 is Rose.

Be aware that some of these numbers do have extra consonant sounds to them. For example, 6 could be "J" for joint but it could also be "Sh", "Ch", and a soft "g" like "gym." 8 is "F" for fibular but it could also be "V." So if I have to create a picture for 86, I'll use whichever one of these consonant sound options that I have for each single digit. In this case, I have chosen a Fish as my image representation for 86. "F" for the 8 and "Sh" for the 6. I then threw in one vowel to give me the picture of the Fish. Spend some time going over the consonant sounds for each digit before moving on.

This is essentially another language that you're learning. This is the language of pictures to numbers. And now that you have an understanding as to how we come up with these images for every number, let me tell you how I went about memorizing these image/number associations.

Many years ago, when I was a satellite TV installer, I would drive around from house to house and during that time I would go over these images in my mind. I chunked them into 10 images at a time and would repeat those several times in order forwards, backwards, and by number. I would quiz myself by asking what is the image for 23, "gnome", what is the number for 67, "jack". I would see the numbers on license plates, on billboards, and on road signs, and I would come up with the images for those numbers. Within my first day of having these images in my head, I was already able to memorize a 20 digit number using this system.

You don't necessarily have to be as manic as I was when I first started and engulf all of these images on your first day, but my biggest tip for you would be to go through them at chunks of 10 at a time until you can comfortably see the images for the numbers without thinking about them too much. The way that I did it, was to link each chunk of 10 images onto my body locations. That way I had a reference point if I had a tough time recalling the image by sounding it out.

Let's start with the single digits

As you know, the location for zero is sand. The picture for "0" is, HouSe. I want you to picture a House spinning round and round on the sand. Visualize the sand going into the house as it continues to spin. Make this image very vivid. Bring it to life. Imagine like it was happening right in front of you. What else would you see, hear, feel, taste, and smell? The more senses that you add to this story, the easier that it will be for you to recall it later.

Now let's move on to number 1. The location for number one is Top, for the top of our head. The image for "1" is a HaT. I want you to picture a Hat on top of your head and the hat is inverted inside out. It's a top hat and you're balancing it on top of your head. Make it weird and crazy. After that, I want you to picture HoNey being squirted out of your nose. Honey represents the number 2 and because it has the "N" sound associated to it, we're going to place that image on our Nose to help us remember it faster. For number 3, I want you to picture a piece of HaM walking across your mouth. Mouth is our third location and ham is our picture for number 3. Add more action to this story. What else would you have the ham doing on your mouth to help you remember it better. Our fourth location is our ribs. I want you to picture an HouR glass repeatedly being turned around on top of your ribs.

Now for a quick review.

What was on the sand? Think about the thing that was spinning round and round on the ground with sand inside of it. It was a House, correct? Good job! So remember that every time that you need to memorize the number "0", just picture a house for that number doing something on a location.

What was on location number 1? It was a Hat. Location number 2 had something squirting out of it. What was that? That's right, it was Honey. The third location featured a food item dancing on it. What was on the mouth? You are correct, we pictured a piece of Ham dancing on the mouth. The ribs are body location number 4. What do we see on the ribs? It was an Hour glass!

Good job on that review. Now, go ahead and place the next 5 pictures on the subsequent body locations. Add a lot of visual connections between the object and the location to help you memorize it better.

Number 5 is HaiL. Attach that to your liver. I would see my liver frozen cold because of all of the Hail inside if it. Number 6 is HaSh brown. Picture your Joint (hip), eating a huge plate of Hashbrowns. 7 is HooK. Go ahead and picture your knee cap being lifted by a pirate Hook. 8 is HooF. Picture a horse's Hoof or horse shoe attaching to your fibula or the side of your shin bone. The last one is 9, which is a HooP. I picture a hula hoop for number 9. So see the ball of your foot twirling a hula hoop around it.

Now go ahead and do a review of the last 5 images that we memorized.

What is number 5? Sound it out at first. You know that all of the single digits start with the "H" sound. The 5 has an "L" sound associated to it. So throw in some vowels and see what you get. The picture for 5 is, Hail.
We linked that to our Liver.

Number 6 is what? See it on your 6th location. What did we picture on our hip joint? It was a Hash brown correct? Number 7 has a "K" sound associated to it. So what is that picture? H_ _ K. The picture for number 7 is Hook. Number 8 is Hoof and we pictured that on our Fibula. The picture for number 9 was what? We saw this one on the ball of our foot. What was going on there? That's right, we the picture for 9 is Hoop.

Great!

Now do one more quick test on yourself to make that you have them all. Say the names of the pictures from 0-9 going forwards and backwards. Then quiz yourself on a random number to see if you can get it right.

What's the picture for number 5? What about number 1? The picture for number 8 is? And how about number 0?

Once you feel comfortable with being able to at least see these images clearly in your mind, let's go ahead and use them to memorize a 10 digit number!

Single Digits 0-9

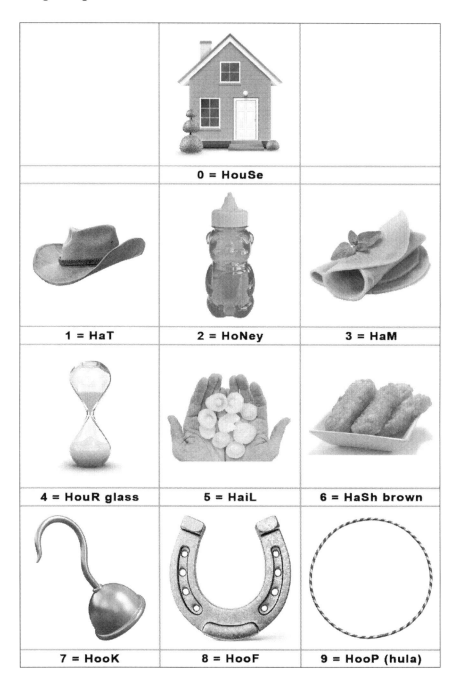

I remember sitting against the fence of a basketball court after playing a few games and telling my friend Edward to give me a 20 digit number. I told him to tell them to me slowly and say them one digit at a time. I also told him to write them down on his phone so that he wouldn't forget them when it came time to test me.

He has skeptical that I could actually memorize this 20 digit number after hearing it just once because he knew what type of student I was in school. Edward and I grew up together and went to the same schools, from elementary all the way to high school. He knew that I had failed several of my classes at Nogales High School in La Puente and it would be a miracle if I could actually do this memory feat.

So he said "Alright man, here goes:
4... 9... 5... 3... 2... 4... 7... 0... 1... 5..."

"Hold on," I told him. "Let me do a quick review."
With my eyes still closed, I took a deep breath and started reviewing the stories that I had just created along my mom's living room. After I felt pretty sure that I had them all down, I told him to keep going.

"8... 7... 1... 6... 0... 2... 1... 9... 5... and 4... "

I took another deep breath, exhaled and proceeded to do one last review in my mind.

"Alright dude, I think I have them all," I said
"No way! I don't believe it man. Let's see. Say em" Edward surprised by my confidence, said eagerly.

"4,9,5,3,2..." I rattled them all off one by one until I got to the last two, "I feel a little shaky with these last ones. I think it was 3 and 4."

"WOW man! You got the missed the second to last one. It was 5, 4, but still this was cool!"

I told him about my plan to compete in the USA Memory Championship in 2012 and he said "I don't know what that is, but it sounds tough. You should go for it!"

You see even though I had missed a digit, I was still impressed at how far I had come in just a matter of days. I learned how to do this "trick" just a few days prior and I was already using what I learned to "show off" but more importantly to show me that the human mind is full of untapped potential. I knew that if I kept practicing, memorizing a 20 digit number would be just as easy as blinking.

So now, let's go ahead and get you going with memorizing your first 10 digit number.

Step 1 in the process is to have locations ready to go in order to create stories along a route. Pop up a set of 10 locations that you haven't used in a day or two. This could be from your home or any other set of locations that you have created, other than the body locations.

Now that you have them ready to go, let's go ahead and take this 10 digit number and place it along the route. I'll give you the number first and then help you memorize it along the route using the images that we chose for each single digit number.

4 - 6 - 2 - 8 - 0 - 1 - 9 - 3 - 7 - 5

On the first location picture an Hour Glass (4) smashing on to it and all of the sand pouring all over the location. On your second location, picture yourself cooking Hashbrown (6) on that location. Remember to add more senses to it. Maybe you feel the location and the hashbrown getting hot. On the third location, go ahead and see Honey (2) being squirted all over that location. Feel the stickiness of that location. Taste the honey that is drenched all around that location.

The next spot will have a Hoof (8). See a horse shoe hoof being tossed onto the location and hear the clanging and banging that it does as it drops onto that location.

The fifth one will have a House (0). Don't just see the house on top of it. Add action to it. I like to personify my objects. So perhaps the house grew arms and legs and it starts to do backflips on that location.

Close your eyes now and do a quick review of the first 5 images that we attached to the locations.

Now create the actions for the next 5 numbers. Hat (1) on the sixth location. Hoop (9) on the seventh location. Ham (3) doing something on your eight location. Hook (7) doing some sort of action on the ninth location. And last but not least, go ahead and see Hail (5) interacting with your tenth location.

The next step is to close your eyes and see all of the 10 quick stories that were created right now.

On a blank sheet of paper or down below, go ahead and write down all 10 of the numbers that we memorized. See the image and translate the image back into the number.

Once you're done with that, go ahead and look back to where I wrote down the 10 digit sequence to see how you did.

Did you get them all right? If you did, way to go! You just memorized your first 10 digit number! That's an entire phone number with area code!

If you missed one or a few digits, then make sure to ask yourself if you added enough action between the image for the number and the location. This is what makes it pop out to you and your brain will more likely remember that visual representation if you add a lot of action to it. Don't just have a static image. Make it dynamic by adding as many senses as you can to the story that you're creating. It's okay to take your time with it right now. The more that you do it, the easier that it will be later on when you want to memorize a 50 digit and 100+ digit number.

To do that though, I wouldn't recommend you stick with just these 10 single digit images. I currently store a 4 digit number on one location. I have memory athlete friends that store anywhere between 6-9 digit numbers on one location before moving on to the next. The difference between what they have done and what you just did right now, is that they have converted more numbers into images. They have a picture for every image between 00 and 999. We're not going to do all of that in this book. I would only recommend for you to do that if you want to compete in a memory competition. It takes a lot of time and a lot of practice to master a 3 digit number system. For now, let's create a 2 digit number system so that you can start memorizing 2-4 digits per location.

> Winners make a habit of manufacturing their own positive expectations in advance of the event.
>
> —Brian Tracy

Chapter 11
Numbers – Double Digits

Let me help you visualize the images for numbers 10-19 using our body locations so that you can more quickly memorize each one of them.

The image for 10 is Dice. Because the ending digit is a 0, we're going to store this on the sand. Visualize yourself rolling huge dice on the sand. Next is 11 which is Tut (king). Picture King Tut on top of your head pulling on your hair. 12 is Tin. You can picture a tin can being shoved up your nose. 13 is Dome. See a dome glass being screwed on to your mouth. 14 is door. Picture a door being used as a plank on your ribs.

Now close your eyes and do a quick review of the stories that we created before moving on to the next 5 images.

The second half of the 10's, start off with Tile as the picture for number 15 and you are going to visualize that on your liver being plastered inside of its walls. The next one is a Dish for 16 and you can visualize a dish plate being cleaned on your joint or location number 6. Number 17 is Tack like thumb tack being pushed and pinned into your knee Cap. On the 8th location, which is your fibula, I want you to visualize a Dove maybe flying onto it and pooping all over it. Add more action to. For example, maybe you get really upset with the dove so you start yelling at it to fly away. Or you forgive it and start petting it as it sits on your fibula (next to your shin bone). The last one will be placed on the ball of your foot or your 9th location. The image for number 19 is a Tub. See the 19 soaking the ball of your foot with water. Notice how it feels now that it is soaking wet.

With those finished. Go ahead and do a review. Close your eyes and see all of these forwards and backwards. Here are the actual pictures for the numbers:

10-19

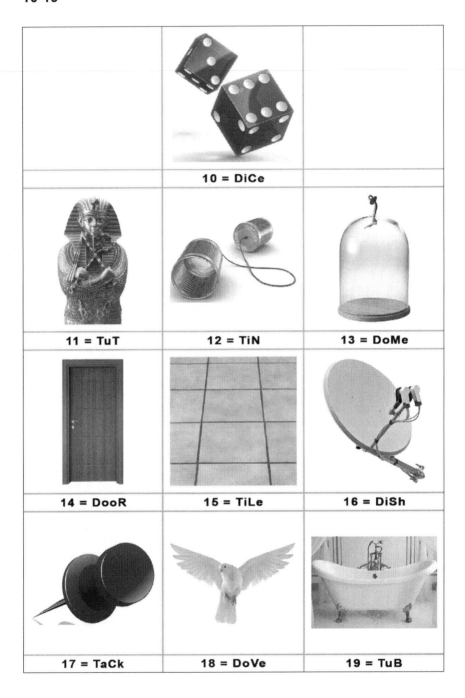

Once you're done with that and are comfortable with each one of these pictures, let's get some more practice in.

Memorize the following 20 digit number on a set of 10 locations. I would recommend for you to use a new set of locations that you haven't used in a few days or create 10 new locations to use with these set of numbers.

12 10 11 14 19 16 18 17 13 15

The first thing that you want to do is store the first two digits on the first location. So 12 will go on that first location which you will see a tin can doing some type of action on that place. Maybe you tie tin cans together and use them as noise makers on the 1st location. Moving over to the 2nd location, I want you to picture Dice for number 10. What do you see the dice doing on that location? Create some strong action between the dice and the 2nd location. On the 3rd location, I want you to picture King Tut for number 11 and he is punching that loci. On the 4th location, I want you to picture a Door slamming on to that loci. The 5th one has a big bath tub pouring water all over it.

Now do a quick review. Close your eyes and see all of the stories that we just created.

Perfect. You now have the first 10 digits memorized. Now go ahead and create the stories for the next 10 digits. Remember to add as much action as you can. Exaggerate it. Make it extravagant. Make the interaction weird, funny, or scary. Add different senses to the stories that you create. Have fun with the process.

The next set of numbers are: 16 18 17 13 15.

It's okay to take your time with each one. You will get faster the more that you do it.

Now that you have that done, go ahead and write down all 20 digits in order on a separate sheet of paper. Then see how you did.

Did you get them all right? If you did, congratulations! You're doing great. If you struggled with a few of them, ask yourself if the interaction between the pictures of the numbers and the locations was strong enough. Don't just see it statically sitting on the loci, make sure that the picture of the number is doing something vivid on that location. I cannot stress this point enough. This is where the magic of the creative memorization process comes into play.

Before we move onto the next set of 10 digits, make sure to do a thorough review of the pictures for the 10's. Go through them forwards, backwards, and by number, several times over. Embed them into your mind. So that if you see or hear that two digit number, you will instantly think of the picture for that number without doing too much conscious thinking.

Now that you know the process of attaching the pictures to the body locations first to get them into our mind, go ahead apply that same strategy to every chunk of 10 numbers. Remember that all of the 2 digit numbers ending in '0' are going to be associated to the sand, the "1's" are on top of our head, the "2's" are on our nose, the "3's" on our mouth, "4's" on our ribs, so on and so forth.

Where is 78 going to go? Because it ends with an 8, it will go on our fibula, correct. What about 35? It ends with a 5 so it will go on our liver. And how about 82? This one will go on our nose because it ends with the 2.

Let's go on to the 20's

20-29

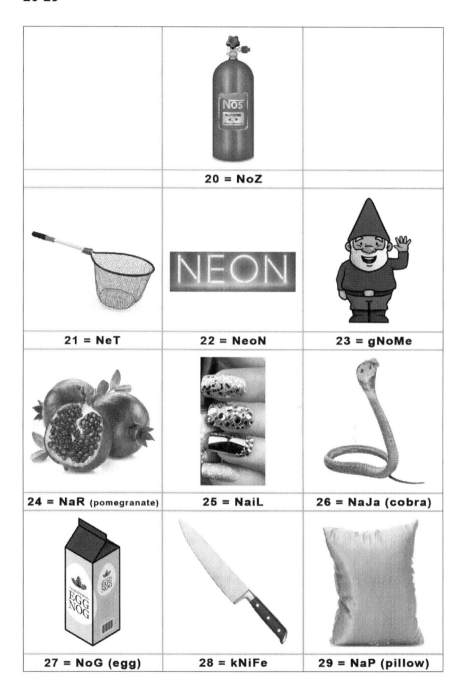

Now go ahead and memorize the following 20 digits on a set of 10 locations and write down the numbers from memory on a separate sheet of paper.

21 29 26 20 25 22 24 23 28 27

Perfect.

Now let's mix it up a bit. Memorize the following 10 digit number using 5 locations and write down them down from memory on a separate sheet of paper.

14 23 16 12 29

How did you do? If it feels like you might be mixing up your 10's and 20's, just take some extra time to review each set several times over in a spaced period of time. They will sink in to your unconscious mind the more that you use them and review them.

Now here are the 30's. Again, link them to your body locations the same way that we have been doing. Also, do your best to get the picture by sounding out the numbers. You already know that the 30's will start with the M sound, so all that you have to do is include the consonant sound for the ending number and throw in a few vowels to get the picture.

If I had trouble with recalling a picture for a number, I used to sound it out and then cycle through the different vowels until one clicked. For example, If I was having a hard time recalling the picture for 39, which is Mop, I would start with the M sound and B/P sounds for the number. Then I would say, Mab, Map? Meb, Mep? Mib, Mip? Mob, Mop? Oh yea, it was Mop!

Usually that would only happen one or two times until it got stuck in my mind that 39 was in fact Mop.

30-39

Now for a practice run with these numbers.

Memorize the following sequence and use your recall sheet to write them down from memory.

38 37 32 30 39 31 33 35 36 34

Awesome. Now let's memorize this 10 digit number.

35 24 16 28 39

How was that one for you?

Are you starting to get the hang of it?

Make sure to take a break after each chunk of 10. Don't do a brain overload. Rest your mind after several minutes of memorizing. Remember that resting your brain is how we actually take things from short term memory into long term memory. Obviously that only comes after taking action on the thing that you want to remember, so definitely continue to practice and then take breaks as needed.

40-49

Memorize and Recall this sequence of numbers

45 49 40 42 47 43 48 41 46 44

Now here's a 10 digit mixture

32 48 28 12 43

50-59

Memorize and Recall this sequence of numbers:

53 50 58 52 59 51 56 57 54 55

Now here's a 10 digit mixture:

45 58 17 30 26

Before moving on to the next half of these numbers, make sure to review all 50 of the first double digit images that we created. Make sure to know them forwards, backwards and by number. Have someone else quiz you. Ask them to say any number between 10-50 and see how quickly you can name the image.

Once you have done that, continue with the second half of these images.

60-69

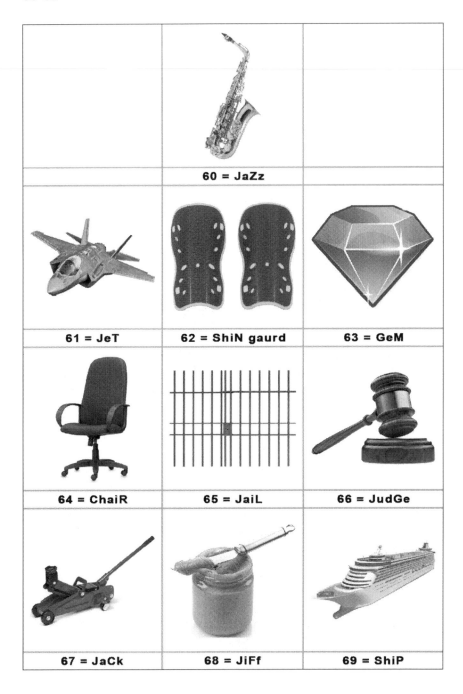

Memorize and Recall these numbers

61 65 63 69 67 60 64 66 62 68

Here is a 10 digit mix for you to memorize and recall

37 64 61 59 12

70-79

Memory Training

Memorize and Recall these numbers:

78 74 79 72 70 77 76 75 73 71

Here's a 10 digit mixture:

57 62 74 19 70

80-89

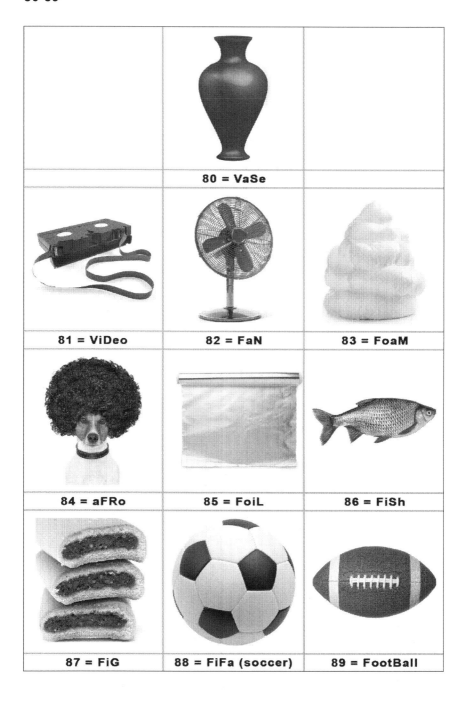

Memorize and Recall these Numbers:

87 82 88 81 89 80 83 85 84 86

Memorize this 10 digit mixture:

61 89 22 85 13

90-99

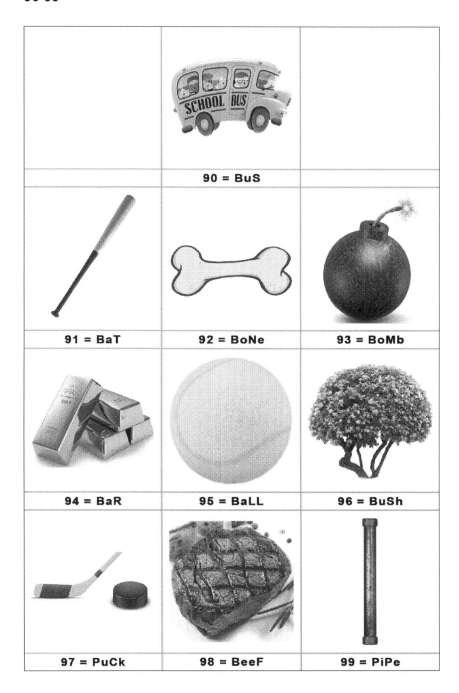

Memorize and Recall these Numbers

92 90 95 99 93 98 91 96 94 97

Now memorize this 10 digit mixture:

98 45 37 91 56

00-09

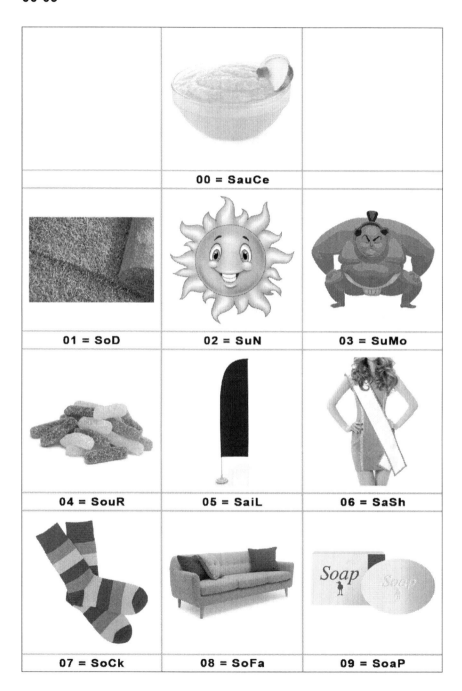

Memorize and Recall these numbers

07 09 04 01 05 08 02 00 06 03

Now memorize this mixture:

08 14 96 67 03

Now that we have finished creating all of the pictures for every number between 00-99 plus the single digits, make sure to review every single number. Practice, Practice, Practice, is the name of the game.

I do two versions of training. My strengthening training and actual memorization training.

During the strengthening phase, I don't actually memorize the numbers, I just get a set of numbers and go through the images if each pair. I picture each one of them doing something right in front of me.

During the memorization period, I actually do memorize a sequence of numbers. I'll start off with a warm up of 20 digits. I will see a randomly generated 20 digit number and I will memorize it in a few seconds. Then I will recall that sequence from memory. I will then up the quantity on the memory training software that I use, which will be up to a few hundred digits depending on how much memorization time I allot myself.

For now, here are a few sequences of numbers for you to practice with on your own. I use a software called memocamp.com and also memoryleague.com in order to train for this numbers event. If you don't want to use that software, you can create a sheet on excel to randomly generate a set of numbers for you.

Number sequences

10 Digit Numbers

A. 9 7 0 8 5 8 8 3 9 7

B. 6 5 3 2 1 4 2 9 7 4

C. 1 8 2 7 6 1 9 2 7 4

D. 2 3 8 1 7 5 6 9 4 3

E. 9 0 3 4 7 1 9 1 1 6

20 Digits

A. 8 7 7 1 7 0 2 4 2 1
7 7 7 5 3 4 0 4 6 6

B. 9 1 8 2 7 2 4 3 4 8
7 4 0 1 8 4 7 7 5 0

C. 5 8 9 5 6 4 6 1 5 8
9 6 3 5 4 5 6 7 5 3

D. 7 4 3 6 7 8 9 9 9 6
6 6 5 0 2 0 1 6 4 3

E. 7 9 3 8 2 6 9 7 0 3
5 5 8 1 0 1 6 2 3 5

30 Digits

A. 0 5 8 1 4 3 2 2 6 4
   5 8 1 9 5 3 2 2 6 2
   4 8 5 4 8 2 4 2 0 0

B. 6 4 5 2 6 9 4 1 8 5
   0 4 7 5 7 4 3 0 6 6
   2 0 5 0 3 7 2 3 8 9

C. 4 9 4 6 3 6 7 0 8 6
   0 6 8 4 1 1 7 4 2 9
   2
   1 3 9 9 7 1 4 8 6

D. 0 2 9 1 9 3 5 5 3 8
   3 7 5 8 3 1 8 3 3 3
   5 3 0 8 5 3 3 1 2 4

40 Digits

A. 7 8 7 0 1 7 0 0 8 1
   2 8 7 0 3 9 4 4 4 6
   5 9 7 8 3 5 7 6 7 7
   7 4 4 9 5 8 6 2 7 8

B. 1 4 4 6 9 7 2 8 4 0
   2 6 5 7 4 2 8 2 8 3
   7 9 1 4 0 0 2 0 8 9
   6 4 3 2 1 9 1 0 6 5

C. 8 7 1 1 7 0 5 2 6 2
   1 2 4 5 5 8 8 0 9 0
   3 1 1 3 5 9 8 5 7 5
   5 6 8 1 0 2 8 8 7 4

50 Digits

A. 5 3 3 7 2 5 5 5 4 2
4 4 0 0 8 2 4 5 9 1
6 8 7 3 6 9 9 1 2 2
8 8 9 5 3 8 0 4 5 8
4 6 7 7 4 8 0 4 9 9

B. 0 6 2 1 3 4 0 5 3 5
9 9 9 4 2 1 3 4 0 3
9 0 8 6 2 4 0 7 6 3
3 9 2 3 0 8 6 7 6 9
2 9 2 5 4 0 0 1 0 5

C. 8 8 2 8 1 3 8 3 6 1
5 1 8 1 1 7 9 1 5 2
9 1 9 6 8 4 3 4 8 1
7 5 7 2 9 0 5 9 5 5
4 1 2 4 2 6 9 8 1 0

D. 3 6 2 2 3 9 3 5 4 7
9 3 5 4 8 6 1 4 6 4
1 9 3 6 1 4 4 0 2 8
9 6 1 8 0 1 1 5 3 8
2 5 5 7 7 6 0 9 4 3

E. 6 1 2 6 1 0 8 0 6 2
0 0 7 4 5 2 7 3 8 1
7 6 3 8 0 8 6 1 9 9
6 2 9 2 4 0 7 4 8 2
4 8 0 8 9 9 4 3 3 9

The most important days in your life are the day you are born and the day you find out why.

—Mark Twain

Chapter 12
Everyday Memory

"Honey can you pick up milk and laundry detergent from the store?"
"Sure babe!"

You get in your car, turn on your radio, back out of the driveway, and head off to the store. On your way over there you're jamming out to your favorite songs on the radio, texting your friends while at the red lights, and thinking about your awesome weekend plans.

You park the car somewhere in the lot, get out of the car, turn on your car's alarm, and walk over to the store. Once inside, you make your way towards the personal care area to buy deodorant for yourself, toothpaste, and cotton swaps. You then go over to the pet section to buy dog food and some doggy treats. You put all of these items in the cart and make your way over to the food section to get bread and peanut butter. You then remember that you needed to get something for your significant other. So you rush over to the cleaning supply section and look up and down the shelves.

"I think that I was supposed to get some type of soap."
You look at the dish washing soap and grab the first one that you see.
"Yup, this should work."

Once you finish paying for all of these items, you make your way outside and then stop.
"ummmm.... Where did I park?" you tell yourself. "Maybe it was this way."

You head over to the left side of the parking lot and start looking around for your car. As usual, it is nowhere to be found.

"I know that I parked it somewhere over here."

You keep looking and about 5 minutes later, you still can't find it. Luckily you have your car alarm activated so you resort to pushing the red button on your key which sounds the alarm on your car when you're near it. You walk another 2 minutes until you hear the alarm go off a few lanes over to the right.

You finally drive off after putting all of the bags inside of the car and head home. Once you pull into the driveway and walk inside the house you hear this, "did you get the milk and the detergent?"

You dash out the door, get back into your car, and drive back the 20 minutes to the store because now there is bumper to bumper traffic on the way to the store.

****

How many times has something like that happened to you? You forget things that you were supposed to get at the store. You forget where you parked your car or even where you left your keys. What about going outside, noticing that it was pretty cold out so you run back inside the house with the intention of getting a coat, and as soon as you walk into your room, you completely blank out and forget what you were supposed to get.

If any of these things have ever happened to you, trust me when I tell you that you are not alone. I used to think that this would only happen to me. That my memory was so bad that I couldn't even remember whether I had eaten that day or not. We are so bombarded with a tremendous load of external non-important things that we lose our focus on the important things that we need to place our concentration into. I'm going to show you how to take the techniques that we have used to memorize random things, and use it to memorize everyday important tasks.

Grocery List

Let's say that you needed to memorize this list of items to pick up at the store:

1. Milk
2. Bananas
3. Oranges
4. Bread
5. Water
6. Toilet paper
7. Soap
8. Toothpaste
9. Dog food
10. Light bulbs

You can do it a few ways. The best way and most effective way is to store it on your locations. For something like this, I usually just store it quickly on my body locations. I would store two items at a time on my body locations. This combines the location/journey method with the story method which I will go over right now.

Let's memorize these 10 things by telling our selves a story with each item connecting with the next.

Picture yourself pouring milk all over a bunch of bananas and smashing those bananas onto oranges. The oranges then get squeezed onto the bread as the bread jumps into a cup of water. The water spills all over the toilet paper which rubs on the soap creating a huge soapy mess. The soap then slides to the toothpaste tube as it squeezes it all over the dog food. There is a bright flash coming from the inside of the dog food bag, so you take a peak to find two light bulbs in there.

As you can see it is one long chain between each item. There is a domino effect of one item doing something to or with the next item in line. You do this until you reach the end of the story. The only caveat to using this method, is that if you are having a hard time with one or two of the objects in the chain, it can be tougher to recall the remaining things along the story. But if you create enough action between each item, then your story should hold up and you will be able to recall the entire string of events.

When I said that I usually combine both of these methods when memorizing a list of things, what I mean is that I would picture the milk being poured on the bananas on my first location. I would then see the oranges being squeezed on to the bread on my second location. So on and so forth.

Another thing that I do, is picture the layout of the store that I'm going to and see myself walking over to each aisle that has the items that I need. I would then see myself getting each of the items and placing them in my cart. When I'm actually physically present at the store, I simply replay back the visual of myself walking through the store that I had created earlier that day. If I think that I'm missing something, I would then do a reverse visualization where I would see myself back in my home looking at some of the things that I might need. I might visualize myself opening up the refrigerator and seeing that I was missing milk so I would go over to the dairy section to get that carton of milk.

Use each of these methods and see which one you like best. You can also combine methods to strengthen the visual connections with the information that you want to remember.

Remember Where You Placed Your Keys and Other Things

In order to remember where you placed anything, you need to have a strong anchor for that particular item. In the case of keys, I like to visualize my keys dancing on the place where I placed them in order to help me remember where they're at later on. If you just toss your keys anywhere without giving any conscious to it, then it will be harder for you to remember where you left them. Ideally, the best thing to do is to always place your keys in the same place every time that you set them down. If that's not an option or you're in a hurry, take an extra millisecond to picture the keys doing something weird, strange, or funny, on the place where you are leaving them.

Remember Where You Parked Your Car

This one always used to get me. I would walk around endlessly throughout the parking lot trying to find my car. When I discovered the memory techniques, this was the first task that I tried them out on.

If I am at a marked parking lot with numbers or letters on it, I create a quick story for them as I see them interacting with my car. One time I was at the mall and parked on the stall that was marked, D52. I pictured a Dog (D) biting a Lion (52) while on top of my car. When I returned later that day, I just asked myself "What was going on top of my car?" Remembering that I had seen a Dog and a Lion on it, I swiftly made my way over to D52. Do this whenever you're at marked parking lots with numbers and letters on them. Turn the letter into an image and have it interact with your picture for that particular number.

If you go to the store, such as Target, and you park near the back left portion of the parking lot, picture yourself doing a cartwheel all the way down to the entrance of the store. What I also like to do is as I'm walking down to the front, I visualize myself exiting the store with the things that I have purchased and doing a funny dance or cartwheel straight back to that left back portion of the parking lot. By doing this, you are future pacing the memory and it will be easier for you to recall where you parked when it's time to actually find your car.

Remembering Appointments, Important Dates, & To Do List

I work with a lot of business professionals such as real estate agents, lawyers, doctors, financial experts, and more. Although all of them have smartphones and can schedule important dates or appointments on their calendars, they still have a tendency to forget about them. I have a doctor friend who would always double book meetings and appointments because he had forgotten about prior scheduled engagements on those particular dates and times. I taught him the following strategy and that mishap has essentially vanished from his life.

If someone wants you to meet them for lunch on Friday, you have to create a story for that specific event. The first step is to turn all of the days of the week into an image.

Sunday = Sun
Monday = Moon
Tuesday = Tooth
Wednesday = Wedding gown
Thursday = Throw blanket
Friday = Fries
Saturday = Satellite

The next step is to take the picture for the day (Friday) and associate it with you and the person doing that action (having lunch) on that particular day. In this case, I would see myself eating Fries at Jim's burgers with Jill while we discuss our business strategy for the next quarter.

If you want to be more specific and have a meeting or appointment for a date in the more distant future, you need to also have a picture association for every month.

Month	Picture	Month	Picture
January	Jam	July	Fireworks
February	Heart	August	A gust
March	Marching Band	September	Sap
April	A Pill	October	Pumpkin
May	Mayo	November	Turkey
June	June Bug	December	Christmas Tree

If the date was November 25th for a dentist appointment, I would see a Turkey (November) using a Nail (25) to clean my teeth.

Another thing that I do to get a general idea as to when I'm free or not, is that I compare the date with something else that I might be doing that week or month. An example of this would be if someone asks me to have a Skype interview with them on Tuesday at 7PM. I know that at that particular time I'm always at Give Back Tuesday feeding the homeless with Living Waters Christian Fellowship in Santa Ana, so I'll tell them to schedule it for 5PM instead. As soon as we lock in the time, what I do is future pace the event in my mind. I would visualize myself doing the Skype session at 5PM and then at 6PM get ready to drive off to pick up the tacos that we donate for the Give Back Tuesday event.

If you needed to memorize a To Do List, you would create a visual trigger for each item on the list and store it along a mental journey. Use locations to memorize the To Do List. Let's say that this is your list for the day of the tasks that you need to get done:

- Clean Car
- Read Book
- Go to Gym
- Pay Bills
- Eat Ice Cream

What you want to do is see yourself cleaning your car on your first location. On the second location, you would see yourself reading and enjoying the book. On the third location, see yourself throwing dumbbells on to the location to represent you going to the gym. The 4th spot could be a bunch of bills all over the location as you throw money on top of them. The last location will have yourself relaxing, eating ice cream, and dropping it on top of the location.

At the end of the day all of this boils down to using your creativity and visualizing the dates and activities that you will be doing during those times to help you recall them later on.

Remembering Street Names and Directions

I once worked on a National Geographic show called Beat the Brainiac. The premise of the show was for a "Brainiac" to compete against 3 "average Joes and Jills" in different tasks. One of my competition events was to memorize driving directions in a few minutes. The three other people could work as a team to memorize the same directions in the same amount of time. They did this task the old fashion way of breaking the directions up into groups and repeating their set of directions over and over again out loud. I on the other hand, looked at the sheet of paper, creating quick stories for each checkpoint, and turned the paper back to the producers in a very quick time. The reason why I was able to do it so quickly was because I was used to memorizing directions. I previously rode a motorcycle and whenever I needed to go to a new destination, I memorized the route ahead of time.

In order to accomplish this, you need a clean mental journey/locations to store all of the checkpoints in the directions. You then take each line of the directions and store along that route. Let's take the following directions as an example:

- Go straight on Main St.
- Turn Right on Rocky Road
- Turn Left on Magnolia Drive
- Turn Right on Stimson Ave
- Turn Left on 32nd Street
- Turn Right on Indian St.
- Stop at 5789 Indian St.

A few things to keep in mind here are that you need to turn the street names into pictures and that you need to turn the directional instructions into pictures. You also need to be ready to use your images for numbers whenever you see them on the list of directions.

In the example above, I would see a Man (Main St.) slapping a ruler (straight) on my first location. Next I would see a Rhino (Right) running into Rocks (Rocky Road) on my second location. The next one would have a Leaves (Left) piling on top of a stack of magazines (Magnolia Drive). The following one would have a Homer Simpson (Stimson) riding a Rhino on my 4th location. On the 5th location I would see a Moon (32) rolling on Leaves. The next location would have and Indian (Indian St.) shooting an arrow towards a Rhino. Now in order to memorize the actual street address, I picture a Lock (57) attaching to a Football (89) as the Indian grabs it on scores a touchdown.

Your assignment here would be to start by turning street names into images. As you're driving around town, look at the streets and make a conscious effort to create pictures out of them. Then instead of using your GPS to get to a new destination, use what I taught you above to memorize that set of directions.

Above all else, guard your heart, for everything you do flows from it.

—Proverbs 4:23

Chapter 13
Accelerated Learning and Education

The biggest pain trigger that pushed me to get into this field of memory training was the fact that I couldn't learn as quickly as other people. I always struggled with being able to focus on the information that I was reading or learning in school. As soon as I got the chance to apply these memorization techniques to school, I did. The first thing that I did was learn new vocabulary words using this system. I then applied it to paying attention in class while the professor was teaching. I also applied the idea of visualizing information in order to stay focused while I was reading new material. All of this helped my take my grades from D's and F's to straight A's.

I will now walk you through some of the different ways that you can apply the memory techniques in order to learn something new much more quickly than you did before. Don't think that you can only apply the methods of memorization to what we're going to be covering in this chapter. You can use this in nearly every subject. The only ones that I haven't quite gotten a grasp on, are the subjects that require muscle memory such as playing a musical instrument. The only tip that I would give you at that point is to practice, practice, practice, and visualize yourself playing at an optimal level after every time that you practice. But other than that, all you need to do is use your imagination to memorize the information that you're learning. Let's go through a few areas of study right now.

Learn Vocabulary Words

Let's say that you needed to learn the following words:

Benevolent = Well Meaning and Kindly
Tawdry = Showy but cheap and of poor quality
Languid = Weak or Slow and Relaxed
Gregarious = Fond of company; sociable
Pulchritude = Beauty
Tumult = Disorder; loud confused noise by a mass of people
Perusal = The action of reading or examining something
Redolent = Fragrant or sweet-smelling
Guffaw = A loud laugh
Abasement = humiliation or degradation

What you want to do as always, is create a picture for the word and then link that to the definition by creating a story out of it. You don't even need to store these along a route in order to memorize them. Just do a direct link between the word and the definition, then make sure to review them over time.

Here are the stories that I created for each word:

Benevolent = I gave my dog a **Bone** inside of an **Envelope** because he was _being kind_ all week.

Tawdry = A **Towel** couldn't **Dry** the wet floor because it was made of _cheap material_.

Languid = On top of a **Lane** there was a **Squid** laying there very _weak and lazy_ like.

Gregarious = Inside of the **Gray Car**, there was a lot of **Rice** _having fun and talking with each other_.

Pulchritude = The **Poker cards** that the **Toad** had were a straight flush which caused a _beautiful_ princess to appear.

Tumult = A **Tooth Mowing** his neighbor's lawn which causes the neighbor to get *upset and yell* at the tooth.

Perusal = **Parrot** poured **Salt** on the book he was *reading*.

Redolent = I used a **Red Deodorant** to cover up the *smell* coming from my armpits.

Guffaw = The clown threw **Golf balls** up in there and they landed on top of his head which made him *laugh out loud*.

Abasement = The guy was shoved into the **Basement** and was completely *humiliated*.

Vocabulary Quiz
Match the Words with it's proper definition.

Word	Answer	Definition
Abasement	_____	A. Fragrant or sweet-smelling
Benevolent	_____	B. Disorder; loud confused noise
Gregarious	_____	C. The action of reading
Guffaw	_____	D. Showy but cheap and of poor quality
Languid	_____	E. Fond of company; sociable
Perusal	_____	F. Beauty
Pulchritude	_____	G. A loud laugh
Redolent	_____	H. Weak or Slow and Relaxed
Tawdry	_____	I. Humiliation or degradation
Tumult	_____	J. Well Meaning and Kindly

How did you do with that vocab quiz? Did you get them all correct? Notice how you were able to think of the visual triggers as you were matching the words with the definitions.

Now go ahead and go through some words that you don't know and practice this technique by creating your own stories. This can be applied to any vocabulary words, from the ones that you get in English Class to the ones that you get in your Science Classes.

Make sure to review them in a spaced period of time in order to move the information from short term memory to long term memory.

Bonus
If a word has an letter in it that I need help with remembering it, I usually throw in my picture for the single letters. For example, if the word was "Blithe," I'll picture a bat biting with leaves on it. The leaves would give me an extra trigger to help me remember the "L" in "Blithe."

Here are the Alphabet Pictures

A = APPLE
B = BALL
C = CAT
D = DOG
E = ELEPHANT
F = FROG
G = GOLFBALL
H = HAND
I = IGLOO
J = JACK
K = KANGAROO
L = LEAF
M = MAT

N = NAIL
O = ORANGE
P = PICKLE
Q = QUEEN (CROWN)
R = RHINO
S = SNAKE
T = TOWEL
U = UMBRELLA
V = VIOLIN
W = WATER
X = XYLOPHONE
Y = YOYO
Z = ZEBRA

Reading and Comprehension

I'm sure that you've had those situations when you're sitting there reading a book or some other material and after a few minutes you stop, look up, and wonder what you were even reading. You have no idea what this book is about. The reason that I found why this happens, is because we're focusing on other things while we're attempting to read. Our eyes are moving from word to word on the pages but there is a cognitive disconnect because we have allowed ourselves to start thinking about something else while trying to read.

What I tell my students to do, is to do their best to picture what it is that they're reading. Not necessarily word by word but just get an overall visual representation for each sentence. What I like to do is pretend like whatever it is that I'm reading is a script to an expensive Sci-fi movie with an infinite budget, and I have been put in charge of creating the actual movie. I have to come up with all of the actors, the props, create the sets, and add any type of CGI animation that will help this movie become the best movie of all time. When I read a book with this mindset, it is easier to come up with the visuals for the information that I'm reading. Try it out with the following passage:

> The wolf was getting closer to Juan's sheep as it crept up on the side of the fencing. It was broad daylight but he was a ruthless wolf so he didn't care if Juan saw him. It had one goal in mind and that was to kill the sheep. The wolf had been terrorizing the area of Gingertown for the last month and all of the farm animals had gotten fed up with the wolf's antics. They had all met up together a few nights prior to discuss how to overcome the wolf's power. They had come up with a plan and were thinking about trying it out the next time that the wolf appeared. As the wolf got closer to the flock of sheep, the rooster started crowing and the sheep charged at the wolf. They formed a line then branched out as they reached the wolf in order

to hit him from every angle. The wolf was so shocked that these sheep would stand up to him that he scurried away, never to return again.

A few questions:

Who did the sheep belong to? _____
What was the name of the city? _____
Which animal alarmed the sheep to charge? _____

Some of the triggers that I thought of as I was going through that passage were obviously the wolf lurking to get the sheep, the rooster coming out to crow, and I also pictured my friend Juan when that name popped up. For the city of Gingertown, I pictured all of the characters near a huge gingerbread house.

Another comprehension tip from reading would be to do a review of what you read after every few pages. Ask yourself questions like who was involved, what were they doing, and what were some of the key points about what you read. Try this out with the next book that you read.

Pay Attention to Your Teacher or a Presenter

The first thing that I like to do when I'm learning something from a teacher, a presenter, or a speaker, is visualize the information that they are telling me as if I was watching a movie. This is based off of the same concept as when you are reading a book. Do your best to create pictures for what they are telling you.

Another thing that I would recommend for you to do is to pretend like you are the teacher and that you are presenting the information that they are teaching. This is called role-reversal learning. Try this out next time that you are in class or learning from someone.

Give Speeches Without Notes

If you want to give a speech without notes or memorize a poem do the following:
- **Bring up some locations to store the information**
- **Turn each main point or line into a story**
- **Visualize that each story on a different location**

Here's an example of a speech:

- Today we are throwing our caps in the air
- Getting ready to go different ways
- To tackle the world head on my friends
- And to start on the very first phase
- Of adult life with all it implies

As you're going through this speech ask yourself, "What can I picture for this line to help me better remember it?" Sometimes all you need is one or two triggers to help you remember what comes next.

Here's what I would picture for each line on each one of my locations:

- Today we are throwing our caps in the air
  - *Caps being thrown in the air*
- Getting ready to go different ways
  - *A highway lane being split into different paths*
- To tackle the world head on my friends
  - *A football player tackling the world and friends cheering*
- And to start on the very first phase
  - *Starting a race on the 1st lane*
- Of adult life with all it implies
  - *A growing adult with pliers.*
  -

Try that with a new speech that you need to give or a poem/song that you want to memorize.

One of the exercises that I do to help me create pictures for key points, words, or lines, is to listen to songs and picture the things that they are singing or rapping about. I close my eyes and visualize the song as if it were a music video but I am creating the scenes for the song. I don't necessarily try to memorize the lyrics with this exercise, it's just a way to stimulate my creativity so that when I do need to memorize something, it becomes easier for me to access that creative flow.

Try that out as well. Then make sure to practice giving the speech several times over and over again before actually giving it.

Learn New Languages

I like using the memorization techniques to learn words in another language. Recently I was in Japan and in China where I competed in their international memory competitions and I wanted to truly put these skills to the test by learning some foreign words. Here are a few of the words and even numbers that I memorized and how you can know what they mean as well by applying the creative story telling technique:

- Arigato (Japanese) = Thank you
    - Elvis playing the Air Guitar while saying Thank You very Much
- Sumimasen (Japanese) = Excuse me
    - Sumo wrestler with a mouse holding an X
- Ni Hao (Chinese) = Hello
    - Knee waiving hello
- Shui = Water
    - Pouring water inside of the shoe
- Xiangjiao = Banana
    - Taking a Shower and smearing a Gong with Gel and a banana

Earlier I gave you 10 static pictures for numbers 1-10. We are going to use those right now to memorize the Japanese Numbers.

The images for the Japanese Numbers are:

1 (pencil) = ichi = itchy
- You're itchy so you scratch yourself with a pencil

2 (swan) = ni = knee
- A swan is on its knees

3 (tree) = san = sun
- A tree is burning up because of the sun

4 (floor) = yon (shi) = yawn
- You're yawning on the floor

5 (hand) = go = go (green light)
- You see a hand on the green light which means Go

6 (sticks) = roku = rocket (w/ goku)
- A rocket ship made out of sticks blasts off

7 (hook)= nana (shichi) = grandma
- Grandma has a hook as a hand

8 (loop) = hachi = hatching (egg)
- Eggs are hatching in the infinity loops

9 (q)= kyu = Q
- The nine looks like a q so that reminds you of kyu

10 (tent) = ju = chew
- Chewing on a tent

You can do this process with any language. Just turn on your creativity gift and use it to memorize the words in the new language that you are trying to learn. A quick example on how I would use it to learn Spanish would be this:

> Picture yourself using a huge Comb to eat your favorite Mexican Food. The Comb in this case represents the Spanish word "Comer" which means "To Eat."

You saw how I linked those two together, right? All that I did was ask myself, "What does this remind me of?" Do this for any language and you will be able to learn it very quickly.

Memorize the Presidents

For the presidents, I have memorized them using locations and using a direct linking to my numbers system.

Here's an example of how this works:

    1 (Hat). George Washington (Washing Machine)

        - Washing my hat in the Washing machine

    2 (Honey). John Adams (Adams Apple)

        - Pouring honey all over my apple

    3 (Ham). Thomas Jefferson (Chef)

        - A chef cooking up a big piece of ham

    4 (Hour glass). James Madison (Medicine)

        - Taking out the sand in the hour glass and replacing it with medicine

    5 (Hail). James Monroe (Moon rowing)

        - The moon rowing a boat on top of hail

The advantage of doing a direct linking method like this, is that once you have a fluent grasp of your pictures for the numbers, you can easily jump to any number and recall that president by picturing the story that we created. The 16th president is Abraham Lincoln. I pictured President Lincoln throwing pennies at a huge Dish which represents number 16.

Try either method to help you memorize the rest of the presidents. See whether the location or direct linking method works best for you. Once you're done with that, start applying the memory technique of creating associations to remember key points, words, people, events, and other such things in your history classes.

U.S. Presidents

1. George Washington (1789-1797)
2. John Adams (1797-1801)
3. Thomas Jefferson (1801-1809)
4. James Madison (1809-1817)
5. James Monroe (1817-1825)
6. John Quincy Adams (1825-1829)
7. Andrew Jackson (1829-1837)
8. Martin Van Buren (1837-1841)
9. William Henry Harrison (1841)
10. John Tyler (1841-1845)
11. James K. Polk (1845-1849)
12. Zachary Taylor (1849-1850)
13. Millard Fillmore (1850-1853)
14. Franklin Pierce (1853-1857)
15. James Buchanan (1857-1861)
16. Abraham Lincoln (1861-1865)
17. Andrew Johnson (1865-1869)
18. Ulysses S. Grant (1869-1877)
19. Rutherford B. Hayes (1877-1881)
20. James A. Garfield (1881)
21. Chester Arthur (1881-1885)
22. Grover Cleveland (1885-1889)
23. Benjamin Harrison (1889-1893)
24. Grover Cleveland (1893-1897)
25. William McKinley (1897-1901)
26. Theodore Roosevelt (1901-1909)
27. William Howard Taft (1909-1913)
28. Woodrow Wilson (1913-1921)
29. Warren G. Harding (1921-1923)
30. Calvin Coolidge (1923-1929)
31. Herbert Hoover (1929-1933)
32. Franklin D. Roosevelt (1933-1945)
33. Harry S. Truman (1945-1953)
34. Dwight D. Eisenhower (1953-1961)
35. John F. Kennedy (1961-1963)
36. Lyndon B. Johnson (1963-1969)
37. Richard Nixon (1969-1974)
38. Gerald Ford (1974-1977)
39. Jimmy Carter (1977-1981)
40. Ronald Reagan (1981-1989)
41. George Bush (1989-1993)
42. Bill Clinton (1993-2001)
43. George W. Bush (2001-2009)
44. Barack Obama (2009-2017)
45. Donald J. Trump (2017-present)

Memorizing the Periodic Table of Elements

I've also done both the location and the direct linking method for the periodic table of elements. I prefer to use the linking method with this information because I can quickly jump to a specific element just by saying the number. 47 is a Silver rock, so I know that the 47th element is Silver. The 79th element is Gold and I pictured a Gold Cup to help me remember that.

Here are the first 10 elements and the visual triggers that I used to help me remember them.

1. Hydrogen (Fire Hydrant)
2. Helium (Balloon)
3. Lithium (Light Battery)
4. Beryllium (Bear sucking on a Lime)
5. Boron (Boar pig)
6. Carbon (Carpet)
7. Nitrogen (Nitrous Oxide)
8. Oxygen (Oxygen Tank)
9. Fluorine (Flour)
10. Neon (Neon sign)

Go ahead and link those and the rest of the elements onto either a set of locations or to your numbers system. Create the stories in order to memorize which element goes with which number. Also, be sure to use your story telling creativity skills to learn and memorize the material in your science classes.

Have fun with this!

Elements

1	Hydrogen	41	Niobium	81	Thallium
2	Helium	42	Molybdenum	82	Lead
3	Lithium	43	Technetium	83	Bismuth
4	Beryllium	44	Ruthenium	84	Polonium
5	Boron	45	Rhodium	85	Astatine
6	Carbon	46	Palladium	86	Radon
7	Nitrogen	47	Silver	87	Francium
8	Oxygen	48	Cadmium	88	Radium
9	Fluorine	49	Indium	89	Actinium
10	Neon	50	Tin	90	Thorium
11	Sodium	51	Antimony	91	Protactinium
12	Magnesium	52	Tellurium	92	Uranium
13	Aluminum	53	Iodine	93	Neptunium
14	Silicon	54	Xenon	94	Plutonium
15	Phosphorus	55	Caesium	95	Americium
16	Sulfur	56	Barium	96	Curium
17	Chlorine	57	Lanthanum	97	Berkelium
18	Argon	58	Cerium	98	Californium
19	Potassium	59	Praseodymium	99	Einsteinium
20	Calcium	60	Neodymium	100	Fermium
21	Scandium	61	Promethium	101	Mendelevium
22	Titanium	62	Samarium	102	Nobelium
23	Vanadium	63	Europium	103	Lawrencium
24	Chromium	64	Gadolinium	104	Rutherfordium
25	Manganese	65	Terbium	105	Dubnium
26	Iron	66	Dysprosium	106	Seaborgium
27	Cobalt	67	Holmium	107	Bohrium
28	Nickel	68	Erbium	108	Hassium
29	Copper	69	Thulium	109	Meitnerium
30	Zinc	70	Ytterbium	110	Darmstadtium
31	Gallium	71	Lutetium	111	Roentgenium
32	Germanium	72	Hafnium	112	Copernicium
33	Arsenic	73	Tantalum	113	Ununtrium
34	Selenium	74	Tungsten	114	Flerovium
35	Bromine	75	Rhenium	115	Ununpentium
36	Krypton	76	Osmium	116	Livermorium
37	Rubidium	77	Iridium	117	Ununseptium
38	Strontium	78	Platinum	118	Ununoctium
39	Yttrium	79	Gold		
40	Zirconium	80	Mercury		

> Find out what it is you want, and go after it as if your life depends on it.
>
> —Les Brown

Section IV
MEMORY ATHLETES

Chapter 14
Memory Competitions

"Neurons on the ready... Begin"

From memorizing cards to committing 1000's of digits of numbers to memory, the last words that a memory athlete hears from the organizers before embarking on the creative journey of memorizing a vast amount of information in a short period of time, are those mentioned above.

Once we begin the process of creating hundreds of stories in our mind for the info that we're memorizing, our neurons are literally firing off at lighting fast speed in order to retain all of that information. We are making billions of synaptic connections every second. As memory athletes we must trust that those neuronic connections will hold onto the information that we're feeding our brains at least until after that particular memory event is finished.

Depending on the memory competition, there can be up to 10 memory events that a memory athlete must train for. They can include: Cards, Random Numbers, Binary Numbers, Spoken Numbers, Names and Faces, Images, Dates, Poems, and even Facts about people. In this chapter I will give you an overview as to how to prepare for the different competitions and what to expect in each one of the competitions. In the chapters that follow, I will dive deeper into how to train for specific main events in these competitions.

When I first got into learning how to improve my memory, I never sought out to compete in a memory competition. I had never even heard about them previously. The sole reasons for wanting to learn the techniques were so that I could do better at school, at work, and in my personal life. Once I saw the huge improvements that I was making in each one of those areas with just a little bit of training, I decided to look further into these memory competitions.

USA Memory Championship

I watched videos online of other people attending memory championships. Individuals like my mentor and 2x USA Memory Champion, Ron White, and now 4x USA Memory Champion, Nelson Dellis, were my inspiration into this world of memory sports. I saw Nelson training up on Mt. Everest as he prepared for a national memory event. He would memorize a deck of cards in a matter of minutes with low oxygen levels because of the high elevations. I saw both of Ron and Nelson square off in the final rounds of the competition. During interviews, several of the memory athletes would say that they learned the techniques a few years prior and were now competing against the best in the nation in the sport of memory athletics. That gave me the confidence to further pursue this new found hobby and attempt to master it like those people were doing.

I looked up the events that I would have to train for in the USA Memory Championship which were as follows:

Main Events:

Speed Cards:
5 minutes to memorize a shuffled deck of 52 cards. Bonus points if you go below the allotted time. You then have 5 minutes take an unshuffled deck of cards and put it in the same order as the one previously memorized. If there is an error in your recalled deck then scoring will stop at that point, regardless of the finished time. You have 2 trials of this event.

Names and Faces (national):
15 minutes to memorize as many names and faces as you can. You are given the first name and last name of each face that you see on a sheet of paper. Currently there are 117 faces that you must memorize the names of. Then the memory athlete gets 30 minutes to recall the names previously memorized. You get one point for every correctly recalled and spelled first name and one point for every

correctly recalled and spelled last name. These are English based names.

Speed Numbers:
5 minutes to memorize the order of as many numbers as possible. You are given 25 rows of 20 digits or a total of 500 random numbers. You are then given 10 minutes to recall the numbers that you previously memorized. You get 20 points for every perfectly recalled row. There are 0 points allotted for any mistake on that row. You have 2 trials of this event.

Poem:
15 minutes to memorize a never before published poem. 20 minutes to recall that poem. Points are awarded based on correctly spelled words, proper punctuation, and correct capitalization.

Finals:
The top 8 memory athletes go on to the final rounds where they compete in a spoken words event, an event where they memorize information about people up on stage, and a double deck of cards in 5 minutes event. The memory athlete that remains at the end of these three rounds became the USA Memory Champion.

I began to train over the course of a few months leading up to the competition. I created spreadsheets for myself with hundreds of random numbers. I shuffled my deck of cards thousands of times in order to practice the act of seeing my pictures for each one of those cards at a faster and faster rate. The event that I disliked training for the most was names and faces. I was just very stubborn and didn't go all in with using the memory techniques to memorize the names. I wanted to resort to rote memorizing them and that's how I trained for names and faces. The USA competition has a poem event, so I got some song lyrics and trained a little bit in this event by memorizing a few lines of those songs.

I wasn't all that structured with my training that first year in 2012. There was a lot of struggle early on. I was also very discouraged because I wasn't getting the results that I wanted during my training. I was seeing the previous records in this competition and I wanted to get close to them. In training I wasn't getting anywhere near those record scores. Instead of memorizing close to a 150 digit number in 5 minutes, I was barely hitting 30-40 digits in perfect recall during that 5 minute memorization span. Instead of perfectly memorizing a deck of cards in 2-3 minutes, I couldn't even get half way through my deck of cards before my timer would go off letting me know that the 5 minutes were up. I needed help so I reached out for a lifeline and some motivation.

I sent Ron White a few messages and he was more than open to helping me out. This shocked me because you would think that as a competitor, you wouldn't want to release your secrets with anyone else. I found this this community is both very competitive and extremely encouraging. Not just in the US, but internationally as well. It doesn't matter where the memory athlete is from, they're always more than willing to share their latest techniques, tips, and new discoveries to help one another out. Ron gave me tips and suggestions that helped me get past my mental blocks. The biggest tip that he gave was to "trust your memory and go faster than you think you can." The negative mental blocks that I was placing on myself was the one thing that was slowing me down, so when he told me that, I felt a sense of confidence surging through and went into the last few weeks of training feeling more invigorated.

March 2012, was my first taste at the world of memory sports. I went to my first USA Memory Championship with wonder, excitement, and amazement. I was amazed to see that there are other people out there who once had a thought of having an improved ability to remember things to now competing against the best in the nation at memorizing quickly. I met Ron and Nelson for the first time. I was also introduced to Brad Zupp who is another top memory athlete. All three of these guys were up on stage during the finalist rounds of the competition that year.

I didn't perform as great as I wanted to. I memorized a 60 digit number, 40 names and faces, a few lines of the poem, and a just a handful of cards in the 5 minutes that were allotted to me, but this was enough to get me hooked. The community was amazing and I pushed my mind to new limits that I never thought were possible.

I have since gone on to compete in two more USA Memory Championships. In each one I performed better and broke several personal records. In 2014 I took a team of high school students to compete in the competition. They were from the Los Angeles area and had never competed before in a memory championship. They ended up getting 1st place in the Team Numbers event.

International Memory Championships

Since 2012, I have competed in memory competitions all over the world. Some I have done really well at and others I wish I could repeat certain events. I competed in my first World Memory Championship with Team USA, Nelson Dellis and Brad Zupp, in London, England in December of 2012. I didn't do so great in this competition, mainly because I only trained for the cards event and the speed numbers event. I didn't take in to consideration the fact that there are a total of 10 events at the international memory competition levels and I needed a whole lot more mental locations to be able to get decent scores in each event. Here are the events at this competition:

1. Speed Cards: 5 Minutes
2. Speed Numbers: 5 Minutes
3. Long Cards: 60 Minutes
4. Random Numbers: 60 Minutes
5. Abstract Images: 15 Minutes
6. Binary Numbers: 30 Minutes
7. Historic Dates: 5 Minutes
8. Words: 15 Minutes
9. Spoken Numbers: 1 digit per second, up to 520 digits
10. Name and Faces (international): 15 Minutes

My best scores in international competitions as of 2016, are the following:

Memory Discipline Event	Score	Championship
5 Minute Binary	216 digits	Tokyo Friendly Open '16
5 Minute Names & Faces	25 names	Australian Open 2015
5 Minute Numbers	120 digits	WMC 2015
5 Minute Random Words	23 words	Taiwan Open Adult 2015
10 Minute Cards	104 cards	Taiwan Open Adult 2015
15 Minute Numbers	176 digits	Taiwan Open Adult 2015
30 Minute Binary	606 digits	WMC 2015
30 Minute Cards	104 cards	Spanish Open 2015
30 Minute Numbers	240 digits	Spanish Open 2015
15 minute Abstract Images	118 points	Australian Open 2015
5 Minute Historic/Future Dates	20 dates	Australian Open 2015
60 minute/Hour Cards	260 cards	WMC 2015
60 Minute/Hour Numbers	462 digits	WMC 2015
15 minute Names & Faces	67 names	Memoriad Las Vegas '16
15 Minute Poem/Text (Old)	52 points	USA 2013^
15 Minute Random Words	62 words	WMC 2015
15 minute Names (national)	59 names	USA 2014^
5 minute "Speed" Cards	124.71 sec.	Australian Open 2015
Spoken Numbers	46 digits	Memoriad Las Vegas '16

My best performance in an international memory competition was the Australian Memory Championship 2015.

2nd Place Overall in the Championship
Gold Position in Abstract Images & in Speed Cards.
Silver Position in Dates and Names
Bronze Position in Binary, 10 Min. Cards, & Speed Numbers

Here are some of the mistakes and pitfalls that I had in training for this World Memory Championship and some of the other international competitions that I have participated in.

Lack of Mental Locations

I had to reuse several of my limited amount of journeys throughout the 3 day competition. What this mean is that I had a lot of interference between the images of the 1st event that I used those sets of locations on and the next images for the 2nd event. For example, If I used my mom's house to memorize several decks of cards for the hour long event, I then needed to use that same journey to memorize hundreds of random numbers to in the hour numbers event.

The solution for this, is to always come prepared with a fresh new set of well trained locations for each event that requires locations. What I mean by well trained, is that don't create a new set of locations at a local Starbucks the day before the competition and expect to be able to use them as well as you would a set of locations that you trained with for several months prior to that event. How do I know this? Take a wild guess. I did just that at one of the competitions and it didn't go so well for me. So what you want to do instead, is to create an abundance of locations that you have repeatedly used during your training days leading up to the competition.

Mentally Prepared for Those Long Events

Another mistake that I made was thinking that by only training for the speed events in cards and numbers, that I would be able to transfer the same results that I was getting into the long events. That is not the case at all. I thought that if I was able to memorize a 100 digit number in 5 minutes then I could easily get 1200 digits correct in the one hour allotted for the long numbers event. Because there are so many more digits to memorize in the long events, you will get mentally drained less than half way through the memorization process if you haven't trained to sit there for an hour straight of memorization and 2 hours of recall.

The solution for this would be to actually train for the long cards and long numbers events. Don't just do the speed events thinking that the results will transfer over effortlessly without training for those events. Leading up to a competition, I would suggest to do the hour events at least once a week for one month. That way you are mentally prepared for the actual competition.

International Names and Faces are More Challenging

In international memory competitions, the names and faces event is much more grueling than in the USA Memory Championship. This is because the names that they use are not only take from names databases from all over the world, but some of them are just way too abstract. It literally looks as if the organizers just jumbled a bunch of letters together to come up with new names. We've joked in the past of calling this even the random letters event. Not all of the names are like that, but they still are tougher than a national competition.

The solution for this would be to practice memorizing names from all over the world. Culminate a list of popular names from different countries, not just the English based countries. Throw Asian based and Russian based names. Take note of the way that names are spelled in different parts of the world. I was recently at the Memoriad in Las Vegas, and one of the names that we had to memorize was "Hanna." Normally, that name is spelled with an "h" at the end, "Hannah." So I had to make a mental note of the fact that this name was missing an "h." The more that you practice with names from all over the world, the easier that this event gets.

Actually Practicing Every Event

At the World Memory Championship in 2012, I went up to my teammate Brad and asked him to help with the upcoming Binary Numbers event because I had never done that one before. 5

minutes before the event started, Brad taught me the system that he used, and I used that to get a better score than I would have other wise gotten in the binary numbers event.

I had never done the words event either but thought, how hard could it be? Well it can be very tough if you're not used to perfectly recalling a list of over 100 words that you memorized in a span of 15 minutes. The issue here is that if you're not used to creating pictures for certain words, then you can easily get them mixed up for other words. For example, if the word was "hiking," I pictured a person walking on a trail. Well come recall time, I would see that visual but I wouldn't know exactly what it was. Was that a representation of the word, "walking?" Perhaps the word was "hiker." Remember that you're supposed to write down the exact same word that was given during the memorization period. If you don't, then you don't get any points.

The solution for this, is to just be ready and spend plenty of time practicing each one of the events. Set up a proper memory training schedule for yourself to get you ready for the competition.

Here is a sample training schedule that I use when I'm getting ready for a competition:

Monday and Thursday
1. Speed Numbers
2. Words
3. Names and Faces

Tuesday and Friday
1. Speed Cards
2. Dates
3. Binary Numbers

Wednesday
1. Spoken Digits
2. Long Cards

Saturday
1. Abstract Images
2. Long Numbers

For each one of these days, I make sure that I do a 10-15 minute meditation session and a 10-15 minute visualization session. I meditate on a clear and focused mind, and I visualize myself having a strong training day and doing really well in the actual memory competition. I also make sure that I my locations are well polished and that I have reviewed them several times over.

I will be going deeper into a few of these events in later chapters and how to specifically train for those events. Let's go right into it.

> If you look at what you have in life, you'll always have more.
>
> If you look at what you don't have in life, you'll never have enough.
>
> —Oprah Winfrey

Chapter 15
Cards

Cards being quickly glided from hand to hand echo throughout the room. The memory athletes look at each one of the cards and attain it to memory. In as fast as just over 17 seconds, you can hear the first timer being stopped by a memory athlete who now has to sit there and wait for the rest of the memory athletes to finish looking at their shuffled decks of cards within the allotted 5 minutes. Once everyone has finished memorizing their randomly shuffled deck of cards, they are placed back into their box and the memory athletes are given a fresh unshelled deck. They now have 5 minutes to replicate the previously memorized deck of cards.

At the Australian Memory Championship in 2015, I was able to get 1st Place in the cards event when I successfully memorized a deck of cards in 2 minutes. During my second trial I memorized the deck in 1 minute but I had a few errors so that trial was voided. Still, 2 minutes was enough to overtake the rest of the memory athletes in this competition and capture Gold in the cards event.

The general technique as to how we memorize cards is the same across the board. We turn each card or set of cards into images and we place them along a route. The specifics as to the images that are created for these cards vary between the memory athletes.

When I first started, I turned each card into one image. I needed 52 locations to memorize an entire deck of 52 cards because I associated one image on one location. I was able to break the 3 minute mark in the speed cards event at the USA Memory Championship using this method. I know of a few top memory athletes that still memorize a deck of cards in this manner. I wouldn't say that it is the most efficient way of memorizing cards, but it is doable. The biggest hurdle with this, is the fact that you need a ton of locations ready to go for training and in competition. If you're okay with creating and consistently using a lot of locations, then feel free to use this method. I'll teach you how to go about creating a one image system right now:

Branching off from the major system with the numbers, you can also associate a letter to each number and suit in a deck of cards. The face cards have different values associated to them.

Here are my picture representations for each card:

S = Spade H = Heart C = Club D = Diamond
Major System equivalent:
S = 1 = T,D Sound
H = 2 = N Sound
C = 3 = M Sound
D = 4 = R Sound

The High and Face cards will have the following values:
10 = 0 = S sound
J = 1 = T, D Sound
Q = Single Digit or H sound
K = An abstract image of your choice
A = The actual suit value

Another way to remember which number is associate to which suit, is to look at the actual shape of the suit. A Spade has one point at the top, so the number is 1. A Heart has two lobes at the top so it is the number 2. A Club has 3 lobes so it is the number 3. A Diamond has 4 points to it, so it is the number 4.

Now, just like with the numbers system, we take the sound of the first digit plus the sound of the second digit a create an image out of them by adding a vowel sound.

Pictures for Cards

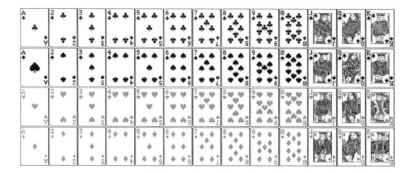

Card	Object
AS	Spade knife
2S	Net
3S	Mud
4S	Rod
5S	Lid
6S	Jet
7S	Cat
8S	Video
9S	Bat
10S	Sod
JS	Tut (king)
QS	Hat
KS	King's Robe

Card	Object
AH	Heart
2H	Neon
3H	Moon
4H	Rhino
5H	Lion
6H	Shin guard
7H	Cane
8H	Fan
9H	Bone
10H	Sun
JH	Tin can
QH	Honey
KH	King's Crown

Card	Object
AC	Club
2C	gNome
3C	Mime
4C	Rim
5C	Lime
6C	Gem
7C	Comb
8C	Foam
9C	Bomb
10C	Sumo
JC	Dome
QC	Ham
KC	King's sword

Card	Object
AD	Diamond
2D	Nar (pomegranate)
3D	Mare
4D	Rear (bumper)
5D	Lyre
6D	Chair
7D	Car
8D	Fro
9D	Bar (gold)
10D	Sour gummy
JD	Door
QD	Hour glass
KD	King's Treasure

After seeing that list of images, you're probably asking yourself if you will get these images confused for the images of the numbers. You won't because there aren't any events where we need to memorize cards and numbers at the same time. I used to have completely separate images for numbers and cards, but felt that merging the two together would cut down on my training time. A lot of memory athletes do this as well. They use the same images that they have for numbers in order to create images for cards.

In order to cement these images into your memory, what I would recommend for you to do is to take chunks of 13 cards, or each suit, and see the images for each card several times until you can do it quickly and effortlessly. Don't try to memorize the cards initially. Just spend time seeing the images for each card. Once you feel comfortable with seeing the images, then go ahead and bring up a set of 52 locations and memorize an entire deck of cards. Take your time with it. Associate one card's image to one location. If it takes you 20-30 minutes to memorize an entire deck of cards on the first try, that's fine. You will get faster the more that you do it. Then what you want to do is take out a separate un-shuffled deck of cards and put it in the same order as your shuffled deck of cards. Obviously do it from memory and then check the order by flipping each card over on each deck. It feels awesome when you see them matching up as you flip over the cards.

2 in 1

Another way of memorizing the 52 cards by using half of the locations with this system, is to associate 2 images on one location. Many of the top memory athletes do a variation of this method. For example, if the first two cards are the 5 of Hearts and the 10 of Spade, I would see a Lion (5H) tearing up Sod (10S) on my window in the living room. I would then proceed with seeing the next two cards interaction on my 2nd location. Normally I would see the first card in that location doing something on or with that 2nd card. This way when I review and recall the deck, I know which card went first and which one went 2nd in that location.

PAO/CAO

Person Action Object or Character Action Object became very popular amongst the community a few years ago. This is where you assign a Person, an Action, and an Object to each card. What happens next is that you take the Person from the first card as it performs the Action of the 2nd card on the Object of the 3rd card. You're essentially memorizing 3 cards on one location.

An example of this would be if you have the 3H, 7D, and KD. The PAO that I chose for the 3H is my friend Feibi Injection a Moon. The PAO for the 7D that I chose was a Dinosaur Breathing Fire on a Car. The PAO that I chose for the KD is Tony Robbins Stomping on a Treasure chest. So now to memorize this sequence, you would see Feibi Breathing Fire on a Treasure Chest on the 1st location.

Here are all of my PAO images for the Spades

Card	Person/Character	Action	Object
AS	Gohan (DBZ)	Slinging	Spade knife
2S	Scooby Doo	Biting	Net
3S	Wall-E	Crushing	Mud
4S	Mickey Mouse	Throwing Fireworks	Rod
5S	Wolverine	Slicing with Claws	Lid
6S	Superman	Laser eyes	Jet
7S	Thor	Hitting with Hammer	Cat
8S	Spiderman	Swinging Web	Video
9S	Batman	Flying with Cape	Bat
10S	Captain America	Throwing Shield	Sod
JS	Spongebob	Flipping	Tut (king)
QS	Sandy Cheeks	Blowing bubbles	Hat
KS	Goku (DBZ)	Kamehameha	King's Robe

I know that the entire process sounds more complex than it actually is. In the beginning it can be, because you have to remember three things for each card where as before you only needed to remember one. But just like with everything else that we have done here, the more that you practice any particular method, the easier that it gets. The pro of this is that you do use a third of the locations than you would with a single object system. The con is that memory athletes sometimes get confused with the people that they imagined on a location. They could see the action and the object pretty clearly, but the person or character might be very fuzzy.

Many times during the memorization process with PAO, I was getting into situations where I would mix the people in my stories because they don't look as unique as say an object or even an action. If you have a friend with long hair as a person for the 5C and another friend with long hair as the person for the 9S, you will more than likely confuse the two when you're recalling the order of the cards. This is because the actual features of each person are not all that unique. Whereas if you have a chair on one location and a flashlight doing something on another location, the features and the interactions between these images are totally unique and different.

With that being said, there have been many records broken by individuals using PAO for Cards and Numbers. I used PAO for a while until I got tired of getting the people confused and switched to a modified version of PAO. I now use PA+O.

PA+O

With this method, I'm memorizing 2 cards on one location. I use the Person performing their Action on the object of the 2nd card. If the sequence is 8C and QD, I would see my friend Nick Dancing (8C) with an Hour glass (QD) on my first location. It's gotten to the point where I only see a silhouette of the person and mainly just jump right into the action of the first card doing something on the object of the second card.

This is what I used to get a Gold medal in the cards event at the Australian Memory Championship. Give it a try if you want have built your PAO system. The cons of this, is that you are needing to use more locations than with PAO but the payoff is that you will be more confident in the stories that you create by using PA+O.

2 Card System

A few of the current top memory athletes are using a 2 card system where they have one image for every 2 cards. This takes a lot of dedication and practice to perfect and master. You need a total of 2704 images in order to have one image for every 2 cards. My goal is to create my 2 card system within the next few months. World Memory Champion, Ben Pridmore and others such as Alex Mullen (World Memory Champion) and Lance Tshirthart (World Record Holder), have used a varied form of the 2 card system. I haven't mastered it yet, so I won't get to much into detail about it now. Once I have spent some time on it, I will surely make a video on how to go about training for this type of system. Make sure to subscribe to my Youtube Channel: AE Mind Memory for updates on this matter.

At the end of the day, no matter what you use, make sure that you work hard at it and train consistently to get faster and faster times. Push yourself and trust that you can go faster. At first you will start off slow, but with consistent effort you will see your times of memorization get better.

A tool that a lot of us use to help us keep track of the memorization time, is a Speed Stack timer. You can get one of those online. Use that to practice memorizing cards under 5 minutes. Then practice memorizing multiple decks of cards back to back in order to prepare for the long cards events in international competition.

A lot of competitions are starting to go digital now. The Memoriad & Nelson Dellis' Memory League Championship do all of the events on a computer instead of a sheet of paper or physical cards. You can train for the cards events and others here: Memoriad.com, MemoryLeague.com, and MemoCamp.com

> Education is the most powerful weapon which you can use to change the world.
>
> —Nelson Mandela

Chapter 16
Words

Like I have previously explained, the words event can be a little tricky if you don't prepare well in advance for it. You get 20 words in each row and you must avoid making any sort of mistake. One mistake gives you half the points and two mistakes gives you zero points for the row.

Here is a sample list of words that might be given in a memory competition:

1. Classroom
2. Steep
3. Both
4. Bathroom
5. Different
6. Hack
7. Introduction
8. Banana
9. Acrobatic
10. Anticipation

There are three words on that list that are pretty visual as standalone images. Classroom, Bathroom, and Banana. You can see and feel these distinct things. Sometimes you might get too comfortable with a word that might be a *layup* and that's one of the words that you end up mixing up with something else. For classroom, you might picture a few desks on your location and during the recall process you might right down just "class" or "school." The only way for you to be 100% sure as to what images correlate with which words, is to use the same images repeatedly during practice for those words. Several desks bunched together with a teacher standing on top of them will signify "classroom" for you. The word "class" could be a student sitting in a desk made of glass. "School" could be a chalkboard and a ruler. That way whenever you see these objects during recall, you will have no doubt in your mind as to what images went with which words.

As far as the more abstract words go, the same fundamental principle applies to them. For the word "steep," I'll picture a long staircase. The word "Acrobatic" might be a crow and bat doing acrobatics moves. The word "different" will be a duffle bag full of rent money. It's all about using your imagination and creativity to come with these silly representations for the words. That's step one in this process.

The next step is to actually memorize the words in order. Most memory athletes memorize 2 words on one location. Some go crazy and do up to 4 words on one location. I would suggest for you to start training with one word per location and then move on to two words.

With the list above, go ahead and memorize all 10 of those words on your locations. I'll help you out with the first 4. Picture a bunch of classroom desks tumbling down a steep staircase on your first location. The next location will see a boat pulling on two bathtubs on your 2nd location. The boat helps trigger the word both as well as the 2 bathtubs which in turn trigger the word bathroom. Finish off the rest of the list by creating either a single association per word on each location, or creating a linked story like I did with the first 4 words.

Write down the words from memory, here:

1. _____
2. _____
3. _____
4. _____
5. _____
6. _____
7. _____
8. _____
9. _____
10. _____

Go ahead and check your answers now by flipping back to the page with the words. How did you do with that? Did you get them all correct? Make sure to practice now by looking up random words online and creating images for them. Culminate a list of 1000 words and create pictures for them. I will share with you some of my sample images for words.

Words into Pictures

add	plus sign on an apple	space	floating in space
ago	a ghost	best	bees covering nest
cloudy	cotton candy clouds	dream	dream catcher
sleep	snail sleeping on a bed	sharp	snake with harp
by	bicycle	present	present with clock inside
advise	addition (blue cross) vase	balance	scale with a ball
abide	a bride	attach	attaching skin with velcro
because	bee case	army	army camouflage uniform
that	teeth hat	abash	A Bush
of	oven	but	butt
clothes	clothes hanger	across	A cross
class	glass desk with "C"arrots	than	teeth hand
mingle	mink coat	retire	rim tire
I	Eye	is	snake
brash	brown rash	abhorrent	ab hornet
calm	carrot poking palm	was	wasp
while	whale	bait	fishing bait
area	pirate with apple on its shoulder	change	coins locked with a chain
there	teeth tire	classes	"C"arrot glasses
unless	underwear	ask	flask
file	file cabinet	with	measure tape
dominant	domino with ant on top	mundane	monkey eating sundae
boon	balloon on spoon	great	cheese grater, great wall
cattle	cat on cows	on	onion
back	spine bending in crazy ways	unit	storage unit
bang	hair bangs	clave	clay cave
yoke	egg yoke	spite	sprite
so	soap	spin	slippery dreidel
who	doctor who	where	white underwear
brass	ball bouncing on grass	flow	flowing faucet
bent	bending a tent	city	sitting on building
believe	bee on a cross	colorful	"C"crayolas making a rainbow
afford	a ford truck	discovered	covered disk
for	ford	approach	happy roach
food	buffet of food	some	sumo
act	action marker cat	dock	duck that's a doctor
action	action marker	bright	brown flashlight
since	sink	we	Nintendo Wii
too	tooth hula hoop	adjust	judge eating apple
cub	baby bear (cub)	yet	yeti
what	water	aunt	ant (red)
plug	pig plugging in an extension cord	shall	shell
brush	big brush	luck	lion holding a clover
alert	Owl, fire alarm	whether	clouds
once	ounce coin	even	oven

> Don't ever let someone tell you that you can't do something, not even yourself.
>
> —Inspired by Will Smith

Chapter 17
Numbers – Binary, New System, & Dates

This has become one of my favorite events. The possibility of memorizing thousands of digits of 1's and 0's is very fascinating to me. The system that Brad Zupp taught me at the World Memory Championship is the same system that I currently use to this day when I compete in this event. It is quite simple to learn and it only takes a little bit of training to get the hang of memorizing chunks of 1's and 0's.

Binary Numbers

This is the basic system for Binary Numbers. You associate a regular nominal digit to a group of three 1's or 0's.

000 = 0
001 = 1
010 = 2
011 = 3
100 = 4
101 = 5
110 = 6
111 = 7

You then take your regular number system and create an image based on the combination of three binary numbers as shown above. If you have the following sequence of binary numbers, 110-100, you will use your image for number 64 to memorize that sequence. 110 = 6 and 100 = 4.

In a memory competition you will get 30 digits in each row. It will look something like this:

101001100010101011110111000010

I know that when you see them bunched up like that, you might get overwhelmed, but don't worry as long as you just take it bit by bit, you will be able to memorize the number without a hitch. In a memory competition you can use a transparency sheet with drawn lines on them to help you break apart the chunks of numbers much easier. I use them in the binary and the random numbers events.

For the number above, the break down for my regular number system would be:

101 001 100 010 101 011 110 111 000 010
 5   1   4   2   5   3   6   7   0   2

51 - 42 - 53 - 67 – 02

Here you can associate one image on one location or two images per location. Just have the first image interact with the second one on the location. I have upgraded my numbers system to use PA+O for every 4 digit number, just like in my system for cards. So my Person and Action for 51 is Wolverine slashing with claws on a Rhino for 42. 53 has my friend Monica using her cheerleading pom poms to throw a Jack (67) in the air. 02 is my brother Chava tying a tie and he would do that on the object for the 6 binary digits on the next line.

I am in the process of updating my entire numbers system into a 3 digit system and doing what a lot of the top memory athletes do when they memorize numbers. They store a 6 digit number on one location by having the first image doing something on the 2nd image in the sequence on the corresponding location. Because I don't want to overwhelm you with having to associate 1000 images for every number between 000-999, I will not include that process in this book. If you would love to learn more about how to do this, feel free to go here: AEMind.com/Numbers for more details.

As for now, go ahead and use your regular 2 digit number system to memorize the following sequence of binary numbers

001 111 110 101 111 010 101 110 000 101.

Numbers - PA + O

If you are now curious as to how to convert your 2 digit number system into a PAO/CAO or do what I do, which is PA+O, I will show you the People and Actions that I used for the numbers 00-09. As you will see, many of them contain personal associations such as friends and family members. Honestly, you can choose any person or character as long as the action is unique. As for the object, I ended up sticking to the one that I already have.

Number	Person/Character	Action	Object
00	Gohan (DBZ)	Turning Super Saiyan	Sauce
01	Captain America	Throwing Shield	Sod
02	Brother Chava	Tying a Tie	Sun
03	Bill Gates	Typing	Sumo
04	Will Smith	Shaving	Sour gummy
05	Black Widow	High Kicking	Sail
06	Michael Jackson	Moonwalking	Sash
07	Friend Jim	Bowling	Sock
08	Friend Lok	Bicycling	Sofa
09	Friend Natalie	On Jet ski	Soap

In order for me to stick all of these new associations to the numbers, I created a link between the Person and Action to the same Object for that number. For example, I saw Bill Gates Typing on the belly of a Sumo Wrestler for the number 03.

If you want to give this system a shot, I would recommend for you to do the same as it is much easier to memorize the references in this manner. Create the PAO for the numbers 00-09 down below then proceed to create all of them for the numbers 10-99.

Number	Person/Character	Action	Object
00			
01			
02			
03			
04			
05			
06			
07			
08			
09			

Dates

Aliens created the Grand Canyon in 1793.
Tortoises learned to fly in 2231.
You became President of the World in 2094.

You will only see these "historical" dates in an international based memory competition. The actual events are obviously made up but you still have to memorize them as if they were fact. You are given 5 minutes to memorize as many as you possibly can and you have 15 minutes to recall the year of each historic event that you memorized. How do you go about memorizing these dates.

The best way would be to have a 3 digit system already created. Meaning you have one image for every 3 digit number. Because what happens as soon as you see the date, you simple take your image for the 3 digits following the millennial/thousands number and associate it to the event. For example if the Year is 1893 and the event is that the Cows jumped over the moon on that year, you would drop the 1 and just see 893 then associate your image for 893 to the cows. If your image for 893 is a Giraffe, then you would imagine that giraffes are helping the cows jump over the moon.

During the recall phase, you will only be shown the events. As soon as you see the "Cows Jumped Over the Moon," you would picture the giraffe, translate that back into the number 893, and add the 1 in front of the 3 digit number to give you the year, 1893.

So what happens if you don't have a 3 digit system? Do you just skip this event? Absolutely not! There are still plenty of ways to do well in this event using a 2 digit system.

One method is to use either Object + Object or PA + Object for the year. For O+O, you would see the image for the first two number in the year, interacting with the second two numbers of the year, as you create a story out of those two images onto the event. If you have the upgraded PAO 2 digit system then you would take the Person and Action from the first 2 digits and the Object from the second two digits as they interact with the event.

Here's an example:

1285 = Oil Waterfall was found in Las Vegas.

For 1285, I would picture my brother Christian (12) upper cutting Aluminum Foil (85) onto the Oil Waterfall.

The second method, would be to use locations to replace the image for the first two numbers. This method does require some prep work with your locations in order to execute it in a timely manner. I learned it from the Australian Memory Champion, Tansel Ali. What you want to do is set aside 100-200 locations. Obviously the more locations that you have, the more dates that you can remember using this method.

Let's say that at the minimum you have 100 locations set aside to memorize dates. What you want to do now, is break the locations apart into groups of 10. The first group would represent all the years that have a 1 after the first millennial number. The second group of locations would represent all the years with a 2 after the first millennial number. You do this all the way until the 10th group, which would represent all the years with a 0 following the first millennial number. The task once you have done this, is to memorize the events and dates onto the corresponding group.

Here's an example of this

1142 = Dancing monkeys learn to salsa.

You would store this on your first group because the hundred's digit number is a 1. So I would see a Rhino (42) dancing salsa with monkeys on the very first location of group one. If the next date is 1136, you would picture that event on the second location of group one.

If the following date is 1473, in which group would you store the event? It would be in the fourth group of locations because the hundreds digit is a 4.

This method does take more dedication to master than just doing a direct link between your images for the numbers and the event itself. In order to memorize the events using the location method, you need to be able to quickly bounce from group to group as you move down the list of events and dates. You also need to create another group of 200 locations if you want to memorize all of the dates in the 2000.

Normally, they include a majority of dates in the 1000's, so you can actually skip around and only memorize those dates. But if you don't want to leave anything to chance and solely rely on skill, I would encourage you to create the location groups for both the 1000's and the 2000's.

Here are a few dates for you to practice with. Use any system that you prefer:

1842 = Dinosaurs built their own houses
2457 = Golf was banned in America
1029 = Yoyo was an Olympic sport
2053 = Steak was ingested in capsule form
1360 = Crackers were found buried in the mountains

Make sure to review the stories that you created and see how many of the years that you can recall:

____ = Steak was ingested in capsule form
____ = Yoyo was an Olympic sport
____ = Golf was banned in America
____ = Crackers were found buried in the mountains
____ = Dinosaurs built their own houses

That's the dates event. You can practice this event in the Memocamp software (www.MemoCamp.com).

> I have not failed.
> I've just found 10,000
> ways that won't work.
>
> —Thomas A. Edison

Chapter 18
Names and Faces - Competition

In a memory competition, you are given both the first name and the last name of an individual. You get one point for every first name that you spell correctly, and a point for every last name spelled correctly. You can omit either of the two names if you're not sure about it or you skipped it during memorization. There are plenty of times where I go through a sheet of names and the last names are so complex and foreign that I only memorize the first names of the faces. That is perfectly fine to do. If you want to truly maximize the score that you can achieve in this event, you obviously want to give yourself the ability to be able to memorize both the first name and the last name of faces provided.

As you know, in the Superhuman show I had to memorize the first name and last name initial of each person. I also needed to throw in there the city and state of where they were from. I created one long chained story for each individual. That's what you're going to have to do with the last name of the person.

Let's say that you are given the following face and are told that his name is Robert Dollan:

What you want to do is create the picture for the first name, the picture for the second name, and have them interact with his face.

In this case, I would picture a Robot playing with Doll's on Robert's eyebrows. If I needed an extra trigger for Dollan, I would throw in some ants to help me remember the ending portion of his last name.

Using that method, go ahead and memorize the names and faces on the following page

First Name and Last Name

Quiz Yourself With the Following Faces

Now quiz yourself here

Now go ahead and check your answers:

Felipe Tafolla
Sierra Carrion
Albert Jones
Richard Smith
Edward Echeverria
Janet Briones
Alissa White
Daniel Johnson
Stephanie Dellis
Melissa Zupp
Jane Hernandez
Mike Williams

How did you do? I know that it was a little more challenging than if you just memorized the first names but it does get easier with practice. If you want to get access to my names training software for free, make sure to send me an email at: LuisAngel@AEMind.com with the subject line: "Names Software."

Remember to Get the book, How to Remember and Faces at www.RememberNamesBook.com

That's it! There are a lot of memory competitions out there and many more new ones are being created every year, so make sure to check which events that particular memory competition is having and be sure to train for those specific events. Regardless of your performance, at the end of the day remember to have fun with the process!

Hope to see you in a memory competition sometime in the future!

> Only one who devotes himself to a cause with his whole strength and soul can be a true master.
>
> For this reason mastery demands all of a person.
>
> —Albert Einstein

THANK YOU

Thank you for going through the Better Memory Now Book! Remember that this is a journey and that one doesn't become an expert overnight. It takes work and dedication. The biggest tips that I can leave you with is to trust your memory (that's what my mentor, Ron White, embedded in my mind when I first started) and to allow your mind to tap into your gift of creativity!

I hope that you found a lot of value throughout this process!

If we haven't met yet, I do look forward to meeting you one day and hearing all about your success!

Take care,

Luis Angel
Your AE Mind Memory Coach

CONTACT

Learn more about Luis Angel's "**Better Memory Now**" programs and other Memory Training material for Professionals, Students, Memory Athletes, and Everyone Else, by going to:

www.AEMind.com

SOCIAL

YT: Youtube.com/aemindmemory
FB: Facebook.com/aemind1
IG: ae.mind
Twitter: @aemind
SnapChat: aemind